ENGLISH ACCENTS AND DIALECTS

An introduction to social and regional varieties
of English in the British Isles

Third edition

ARTHUR HUGHES

Senior Lecturer in Linguistic Science, University of Reading

PETER TRUDGILL

Professor of English Linguistics, Université de Lausanne

ARNOLD

A member of the Hodder Headline Group
LONDON • NEW YORK • SYDNEY • AUCKLAND

First published in Great Britain in 1996 by
Arnold, a member of the Hodder Headline Group
338 Euston Road, London NW1 3BH
175 Fifth Avenue, New York, NY10010

Distributed exclusively in the USA by
St Martin's Press Inc.,
175 Fifth Avenue,
New York, NY 10010

British Library Cataloguing in Publication Data
A catalogue entry for this book is available from the British Library

Library of Congress Cataloging-in-Publication Data
Hughes, Arthur. 1941–
    English accents and dialects: an introduction to social and regional varieties of
English in the British Isles / Arthur Hughes, Peter Trudgill. — 3rd ed.
        p.   cm.
    Includes bibliographical references and index.
    ISBN 0–340–61445–5 (pb). — ISBN 0–340–61446–3 (cassette)
    1. English language—Social aspects—Great Britain.   2. English language—
Variation—Great Britain.   3. English language—Dialects—Great
Britain.   4. English language—Great Britain.   I. Trudgill, Peter.   II. Title.
PE1711.H8   1996
427'.941–dc20   96–11677

ISBN 0 340 61445 5(Pb)

This book is accompanied by a recording, which is available on cassette only.

Composition by J&L Composition Ltd, Filey
Printed and bound in Great Britain by JW Arrowsmith Ltd, Bristol.

Contents

Acknowledgements

A very large number of people have helped us with this book, and we can acknowledge only some of them here. Over the years we have profited enormously from discussions on varieties of English with G. O. Knowles and J. C. Wells, and we are also very grateful to Peter Bedells, Viv Edwards, Sandra Foldvik, Erik Fudge, Vicky Hughes, Sandy Hutcheson, Elspeth Jones, Robin McClelland, Suzanne McClelland, James Milroy, Lesley Milroy, K. M. Petyt, and David Sutcliffe, who have provided us with information on specific points (sometimes without realizing it) and have corrected some of our worst misapprehensions. We would also like to thank all those people, many of whom went to a very great deal of trouble on our behalf, and some of whom prefer to remain anonymous, who helped us with the tape-recordings. We would particularly like to acknowledge the assistance in this respect of Margaret Ainsbury, Tony Beard, Gillian Brown, Ray Brown, Edwin Cannon, Joy Cannon, Chris Connor, Roseanne Cook, Karen Currie, Fergus Daly, Sally Davies, Geoffrey Dearson, Angela Edmondson, Kirsty Evans, Anne Fenwick, Stanley Fletcher, Milton Greenwood, Isabel Holmes, David Holmes, Kathy Holmes, Carl James, Daisy James, Toni Johnson, Wilf Jones, Paul Kerswill, Gillian Lane-Plescia, Chris Lawrence, Catherine Lovell, Gillian Lovell, Caroline Macafee, Bridie McBride, Helen Mattacott, Jackie Mountford, Grahame Newell, Kristyan Spelman Miller, Enid Warnes, Gwyn Williams and, especially, Euan Reid. And, finally, we are very grateful indeed to R. W. P. Brasington, J. K. Chambers, Paul Fletcher, Michael Garman, Hanne Svane Nielsen and F. R. Palmer, who read earlier versions of the book and made many valuable suggestions for improvement.

Shetland
Islands

Orkney
Islands

'Lowland
Scots'

Edinburgh

Glasgow

Northumberland

Belfast

Bradford

Liverpool

Dublin

Walsall

Norwich

Pontypridd

London

Bristol

Devon

Map 1

Symbols

Vowel charts

To indicate the quality of vowels, we make use in the text of cardinal vowel charts. A vowel is assigned a position on two dimensions: open v close, and front v back, and this position corresponds roughly to the position in the mouth of the highest point of the tongue in the production of that vowel. Presence or absence of lip rounding is shown by choice of symbol. Diacritics are used to give more precise indication of vowel quality. For a fuller account of the cardinal vowel system, see O'Connor (1973).

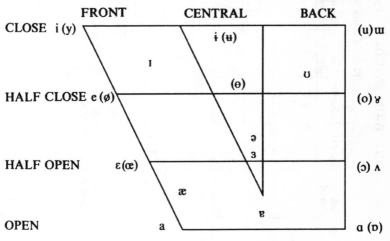

Parentheses indicate symbols representing vowels with lip rounding

Diacritics
- ┬ more open
- ├ retracted
- ·· centralized
- : long
- . half long
- ˌ stress

Consonant symbols used in the book[1]

Place of articulation

Manner of articulation	Bilabial	Labio-dental	Dental	Alveolar	Post-alveolar	Palato-alveolar	Retroflex	Palatal	Velar	Labio-velar	Uvular	Glottal
Plosive	p b			t d					k g			ʔ
Fricative	ɸ	f v	θ ð	s z		š ž		ç	x			h
Affricate						č ǰ						
Nasal	m	ɱ		n					ŋ			
Approximant		ʋ			ɹ		ɻ	j		ʍ w	ʁ	
Lateral			l ɬ									
Tap/Flap				ɾ								

[1] Most of the sounds represented in this table are described in Chapter 3. The others are described in Chapter 5.
Note Where two symbols are placed one above the other within a cell, the upper symbol represents a voiceless sound and the lower symbol represents a voiced sound.

Diacritics
syllabic ņ ḷ
dental t̪
aspirated pʰ
voiceless n̥

Word List

Words used in the recordings
(with RP pronunciation)

1 pit /pɪt/	19 city /sɪtɪ/	36 fur /fɜ:/
2 pet /pɛt/	20 seedy /si:dɪ/	37 fair /fɛə/
3 pat /pæt/	21 hat /hæt/	38 nose /nouz/
4 put / pʊt/	22 dance /dɑ:ns/	39 knows nouz/
5 putt /pʌt/	23 daft /dɑ:ft/	40 plate / pleit/
6 pot /pɒt/	24 half /hɑ:f/	41 weight /weit/
7 bee /bi:/	25 father /fɑ:ðə/	42 poor /pʊə/
8 bay /bei/	26 farther /fɑ:ðə/	43 pour /pɔ:/
9 buy /bai/	27 pull /pʊl/	44 pore /pɔ:/
10 boy /bɔi/	28 pool /pu:l/	45 paw /pɔ:/
11 boot /bu:t/	29 pole /poul/	46 tide /taid/
12 boat /bout/	30 Paul /pɔ:l/	47 tied /taid/
13 bout /baut/	31 doll /dɒl/	48 pause /pɔ:z/
14 beer /bɪə/	32 cot /kɒt/	49 paws /pɔ:z/
15 bear /bɛə/	33 caught /kɔ:t/	50 meet /mi:t/
16 bird /bɜ:d/	34 fir /fɜ:/	51 meat /mi:t/
17 bard /bɑ:d/	35 fern /fɜ:n/	52 mate /meit/
18 board /bɔ:d/		

Note that the relatively young reader of the word list on the cassette has /bɛ:/ for *bear* and /pɔ:/ for *poor*.

|1|

Variation in English

When foreign learners of English first come to the British Isles, they are usually surprised (and dismayed) to discover how little they understand of the English they hear. For one thing, people seem to speak faster than expected. For another, the English that most people speak seems to be different in many ways from the English they have learned. While it is probably differences of pronunciation that will immediately strike them, learners may also notice differences of grammar and vocabulary.

Their reaction to this experience will vary. If they are confident in their own and their teachers' ability, they may conclude that most of the English (and Welsh, Scottish, and Irish) people that they hear cannot, or at least do not, speak English correctly. In this they would find many native speakers to agree with them. Indeed, there would even be some who would tell them that, since they have *studied* the language, they should know better what is correct.

We shall deal in two ways with the suggestion that native speakers cannot speak their own language correctly. Firstly, we can point out that for learners visiting Britain the question of correctness is largely irrelevant. Their problem is to understand what they hear, regardless of whether it is correct or not. And the description and analysis of variation provided in this book, together with the tape recordings, is an attempt to help them do this. They should also help them decide which features of what they hear they can safely integrate into their own speech. The second thing we can do is to try to show that the notion of 'correctness' is not really useful or appropriate in describing the language of native speakers. We shall not do this immediately, but when examples of what might be considered incorrect English arise.

Another reaction on the part of learners to their failure to understand what is said may be to think that perhaps what they learned in their own country was not 'real' English. Happily, nowadays this is unlikely to be the case. But, although the English they have learned is real enough, it will tend to be limited to a single variety of the language, one chosen to serve as a model for their own speech. It will usually be the speech of a particular group of native speakers as it is spoken, slowly and carefully, in rather formal situations. Given limitations of time, of teachers' knowledge, and of students' aspirations and attitude, this restriction is entirely reasonable, at least as far as speaking is concerned. Learners, though they may sound somewhat odd at times, will usually be able to make themselves understood. But such a restriction as far as listening comprehension is concerned is less easily justified. While native speakers may be able to 'decode' the learners' messages, they do not generally have the ability, or the inclination to 'encode' their own messages in a form comprehensible to learners. In many cases, of course, they will simply not be aware of the difficulty. Even when they are, their most common strategy will be to repeat what has just been said, only louder, or to revert to 'foreigner talk' (me come, you go – savvy?), usually making understanding even more difficult. It seems to us, therefore, that exposure to a number of varieties of English, and help in understanding them, can play an important and practically useful part in the study of English as a foreign language.

Even when learners with comprehension problems recognize that English, like their own language, indeed like every language, is subject to variation, so complex and at times so subtle is that variation that it is usually a long time before they begin to see much order in it. And native speakers, even those who teach the language, are often hard put to explain the things that puzzle them. For this reason, we shall attempt now to give some idea of the principal ways in which British and Irish English speech varies and, just as important, the non-linguistic factors which condition that variation. It is hoped by doing this to provide a framework in which to set the features of social and regional variation, which will be our main concern in the remainder of the book, and to show how they are related to other types of variation.

Variation in pronunciation

RP

We must first make clear the way we are going to use two important terms, 'dialect' and 'accent'. We shall use DIALECT to refer to varieties distinguished from each other by differences of grammar and vocabulary. ACCENT, on the other hand, will refer to varieties of pronunciation. The reason for making this distinction will become apparent as the chapter proceeds.

Whenever British rather than, say, American English is taught, the accent presented as a model for the learner will almost always be 'received pronunciation', or 'RP'. 'Received' here is to be understood in its nineteenth-century sense of 'accepted in the best society'. While British society has changed much since that time, RP has nevertheless remained the accent of those in the upper reaches of the social scale, as measured by education, income and profession, or title. It is essentially the accent of those educated at public schools (which are of course private, and beyond the means of most parents). It is largely through these schools that the accent is perpetuated. For RP, unlike prestige accents in other countries, is not the accent of any region (except historically: its origins were in the speech of London and the surrounding area). It is quite impossible to tell from pronunciation alone where an RP speaker comes from.

It has been estimated that only about three per cent of the English population speak RP (see Trudgill, 1979). Why, then, is it the accent taught to foreign learners? Its prestige has already been mentioned. No doubt learners want to learn, and teachers to teach, the 'best' accent, and for most British people, because they associate the accent with the high social status of its speakers, RP is the best and even the most 'beautiful' accent. There is another reason, however, for learning RP. If we were asked to point to a readily available example of RP, we would probably suggest the speech of BBC newsreaders. Because of its use on radio and television, within Britain RP has become the most widely understood of all accents. This in turn means that the learner who succeeds in speaking it, other things being equal, has the best chance of being understood. Another good reason for learning RP is that it is by far the most thoroughly described of British accents. This is the case, at least in part, because descriptions of it were made in response to the needs of foreign learners and their teachers. We describe the sounds of RP in Chapter 3.

Language change

Learners who have been presented with RP as a model should not think, when they come to Britain, that speech they hear which is in some way different from that model is necessarily not RP. First, accents, like all components of living languages, change with time. In RP, for example, there is a tendency at present for certain triphthongs and diphthongs to become monophthongs. Thus the word *tyre*, which was once most commonly pronounced /taɪə/ (triphthong), came to be pronounced /taə/ (diphthong), and is now increasingly reduced to /tɑ:/ (monophthong, with the same pronunciation as the word *tar*). These changes with time can be seen reflected to some degree in the pronunciation of speakers of different ages. Young people, most particularly those of the highest social class and educated at the most prestigious public schools, will tend to say /tɑ:/; those somewhat older will tend to say /taə/; and there will be others, older still, who will say /taɪə/. Of course there is not a perfect correlation between age and pronunciation. Some RP speakers, including the young, will regard the distinguishing features of the advanced variety of the accent (see p. 37) as 'affected' and not alter their own speech, at least not until, with the passage of time, the adoption of these features becomes more general. Other RP speakers will be only too ready to integrate them into their own speech.

Which variety of RP is taught will differ from country to country, indeed from classroom to classroom. What learners of advanced RP should bear in mind is that this form of pronunciation does sound affected to most British people, and that, if they acquire it successfully, even though their listeners are aware that they are foreigners, their speech may sound affected too. For many people with regional accents all RP speech, however conservative, sounds affected, and the supposed affectation is felt most strongly at those points where the differences between RP and the regional accent of the listener are most marked.

Stylistic variation

As we have just seen, there are differences of pronunciation among RP speakers. There is, in addition, variation in the pronunciation of individual RP speakers. Most trivially, studies in instrumental phonetics have shown that a person cannot produce even a single sound in exactly the same way twice in succession. And it is obvious that people with food in their mouths, or who have just drunk eight pints of beer, will not speak in quite the same way as in other circumstances. But what is more significant for us are the changes in pronunciation made, consciously or unconsciously, by speakers according to their perception of the situation in which they find themselves, especially how formal or informal they feel it to be. Their judgement of formality will depend on a number of factors, such as the relative status of the people they are talking to, how well they know each other, what they are talking about, to what purpose and in what place. Some idea of the range of formality can be given by listing just a few of the terms for occasions on which words are uttered – proclamation, lecture, consultation, conversation, chat. In what speakers see as a very formal situation they will tend to articulate more slowly and carefully. Individual sounds will be given their full value; none will be omitted. In a very informal situation, on the other hand, they will be more likely to speak quickly, less carefully, and some sounds will either have their value changed or be omitted entirely. Thus the word *are* may be pronounced /ɑː/ in deliberate speech, but (when unstressed) will become /ə/ in more casual speech (this process being known as vowel weakening); /ðæt pleit/ (*that plate*) will become /ðæp pleit/ (assimilation); /ɪkspˈɛkt souʊ/ (*expect so*) will become /kspˈɛk souʊ/ (elision). Variation conditioned in this way by people's perception of the situation in which they are speaking we refer to as 'stylistic'.

It should not be thought that a more casual style of pronunciation is in any sense incorrect. It is really not a matter of correctness, but of appropriateness. It would be odd, even ridiculous, for a radio commentator to use the same style of pronunciation when telling his girlfriend how desirable she is, as when describing for his listeners a royal procession. It is just possible nevertheless that there are radio commentators who would do this, for it is not only situational factors which determine style of pronunciation, but also the speaker's personality. Some people are very sensitive to what they regard as the demands of a situation on their speech style, while others appear indifferent, speaking with little change of pronunciation in the widest range of situations. Some of those who always speak carefully and with great deliberation maintain that to do anything else is 'slovenly', 'sloppy', and leads to loss of clarity and to possible misunderstanding. In this claim they forget how much of language is redundant. There is usually far more information in an utterance than we need in order to understand it. The small loss in information resulting from modifications in pronunciation of the kind exemplified above rarely causes confusion: /ɪksp'ɛk sou/ can only be *expect so*. Even where linguistically there is ambiguity, the situation will normally disambiguate: if we are asked if we would like some /mɪns/, we can infer without too much difficulty from the proffered rattling bag that the offer is of *mints* and not *mince* (meat). And if we were not sure, in an informal situation it would be perfectly natural to ask which was intended.

As has been said before, whatever learners think about this kind of thing, their task is to understand what is said. Unfortunately, it is a task for which they are not always well prepared. Language teachers, like all of us, want to be understood, and are inclined to speak slowly and with deliberation, a tendency in which they are not discouraged either by their students or by the often formal atmosphere of the classroom. Learners may be familiar with such processes as vowel weakening, assimilation and elision, but they usually have little idea of the degree to which they occur in ordinary conversational English. Even the tape-recorded conversations of native speakers marketed commercially tend to sound rather stiff and stilted. The need for recordings of speech of a more spontaneous nature has been recognized, however, and some are available (Crystal and Davy, 1975).

Unconditioned variation

Within RP there are differences of pronunciation which cannot be explained in terms either of a change taking place or of speech style. Examples are the pronunciation of *economic* as /iːkənˈɒmɪk/ or /ɛkənˈɒmɪk/. Speakers will have a preference for one over the other, and all that we can usefully say is that some people, perhaps a majority, say this and others say that.

Regional variation

As we have seen, only a very small percentage of the population of England speak RP. The others have some form of regional accent. Much of Chapter 4 is concerned with regional accents, and we shall do no more here than make some general observations.

Regional accents are sometimes spoken of as, for instance, northern or southern English, Irish, or Welsh. But this is not to say that there is, for example, one Irish or one north of England accent. It means only that speakers in one of those areas, say the north of England, have enough pronunciation features in common with each other, which are not shared with speakers of other areas, for us to say of someone we hear speaking 'He's from the north.' Just as 'northern accent' is no more than a convenient label for a group of more local accents, something like 'Yorkshire accent' is simply a label for a group of accents which are even more local. Almost however small an area we look at, we will find differences between the pronunciation there and an area adjoining it. At the same time, unless there is some considerable obstacle to communication between the two areas, those differences will be so slight that we should be unhappy about drawing a line between them and saying that on one side of the line the accent was X and that on the other it was Y. In Britain, from the south-west of England to the north of Scotland we do not have a succession of distinct accents, but a continuum, a gradual changing of pronunciation. In order to describe regional variation, however, it is convenient at times to speak of accents as if they were entities to be found within certain defined limits, and from now on this is what we shall do.

Speakers of RP are at the top of the social scale, and their speech gives no clue to their regional origin. People at the bottom of the social scale speak with the most obvious, the 'broadest' regional accents. Between these two extremes, in general (and there are always individual exceptions) the higher people are on the social scale, the less regionally marked will be their accents, and the less they will differ from RP. This relationship between class and accent can be represented diagrammatically in the form of a triangle:

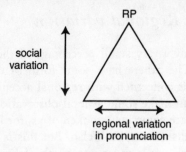

Figure 1.1

This relationship between accent and the social scale can be illustrated with figures for 'aitch-dropping' (say, for example, /æt/ instead of /hæt/) in the Bradford area of Yorkshire (Petyt, 1977):

	% aitches dropped
Upper middle class	12
Lower middle class	28
Upper working class	67
Middle working class	89
Lower working class	93

Not all people stay in one social position throughout their lives. Those who climb the social scale will tend to modify their accent in the direction of RP, thereby helping to maintain the existing relationship between class and accent. Speakers with a Bradford accent would begin to pronounce more aitches. They might try, too, to introduce the vowel /ʌ/, absent from northern English accents but which in RP distinguishes *putt* /pʌt/ from *put*/ /pʊt/. But to do this is not easy. It means dividing all those words which in the north of England contain the vowel /ʊ/ into two groups according to their pronunciation in RP. What often happens is that some words which have /ʊ in RP as well as in the regional accent are wrongly classified, and so *cushion* /kˈʊšn̩/ in both accents, is pronounced /kˈʌsn̩/. This is referred to as hypercorrection (see p. 55).

In view of what has just been said, it is not surprising that there seems to be greater variation in the speech of individual speakers of modified regional accents than in that of RP speakers. In what individual speakers regard as a formal situation, particularly in the company of RP speakers, they will probably not only attempt to make their speech more like RP, but, since they effectively are learners of RP, they will also speak more slowly and carefully in order to avoid making mistakes.

It is sometimes said that nowadays there is not the same pressure as there once was to modify one's speech in the direction of RP. Reference is made to the fact that announcers with non-RP accents are now to be heard on the BBC, that important posts in industry and the civil service are held by non-RP speakers, and that some younger RP speakers have adopted, more or less deliberately, features of regional pronunciation. Perhaps the pressure is less, but it is still there. In an experiment carried out in South Wales, a university lecturer, introduced as such, gave the same talk, word for word, to two matched groups of schoolchildren aged 16 to 18 years (Giles *et al.*, 1975). The only difference between the two talks was the accent. He addressed one group in RP, the other in a Birmingham accent. When the schoolchildren were then asked to evaluate the lecturer according to a number of criteria, those who had heard him speak RP gave him a significantly higher rating of intelligence than the group who had heard him use a Birmingham accent. It is true that some people appear most unwilling, despite changes in their social status, to modify their regional accent, and that certain regional accents (including some Scottish) are more prestigious and felt to require less modification than others. It is probable, however, that, if only by contact with more RP speakers, there is some modification of pronunciation attendant on social advancement.

Grammatical and lexical variation

Standard English

The term ACCENT, as we have seen, refers to varieties of pronunciation. The term DIALECT, on the other hand, at least as we shall use it here, refers to varieties distinguished from each other by differences of grammar and vocabulary. With British English, though not with all other languages, the separation of accent from dialect is not only logically possible but almost required by the relationship that holds between them. The accent taught to foreign learners of British English is RP. The dialect used as a model is known as 'Standard English', the dialect of educated people throughout the British Isles. It is the dialect normally used in writing, for teaching in schools and universities, and heard on radio and television. Unlike RP, Standard English is not restricted to the speech of a particular social group. While it would be odd to hear an RP speaker consistently using a non-standard dialect of English, most users of Standard English have regional accents. What social variation there is within Standard English appears to be limited to a rather small number of lexical items, the choice of the word *serviette* rather than (table) *napkin*, for example, indicating inferior social standing.

Another way in which Standard English differs from RP is that it exhibits some regional variation. Subsumed under Standard English (or Standard British English) are Standard English English (in England and Wales), Standard Scottish English, and Standard Irish English. In Scotland and Ireland there are regional features which, because they are to be found regularly even in formal writing, are considered 'standard'. In Standard Scottish English, for example, we find 'They hadn't a good time' rather than the Standard English English, 'They didn't have a good time.' It is of course usually the latter which is taught to foreign students. Variation between these standard dialects is in fact quite limited, and should cause learners no problems.

Language change

The grammar of a dialect changes with time, but very slowly. Grammatical forms and structures, members of tightly knit, closed systems, resist alteration, and it is not easy to identify ongoing grammatical development.

One interesting example of grammatical variation which may represent the beginning of a change in the language is the apparently increasing use of the 'present perfect' in conjunction with expressions of definite past time reference. One hears such things as 'And Roberts has played for us last season' (without any kind of break). Most native speakers, it must be admitted, would find this odd. They would claim that the speaker had made a mistake. But sentences like this are heard more and more often. The captain of a cricket team who said 'And Roberts has played for us last season' had been asked about the present strength of his side. His answer combined an indication of the current relevance of Roberts' having played with the information that it was in the previous season that he had played. In this way he said in one sentence what can normally only be said in two: 'Roberts has played for us. He played last season'. It is not at all certain that the use of this grammatical device will continue to increase. For the time being it will be regarded as a mistake. But if eventually it becomes generally accepted (just as previously 'incorrect' sentences like 'The house is being built next spring' are now accepted as good English), then it will be yet another subtlety for foreign learners to master, in an area which is already difficult enough.

Lexical change is more rapid than grammatical change. It is easier to see the variation that sometimes accompanies it. In some cases a new lexical item enters the language and displaces one already there. In this way *record player* has largely taken the place of *gramophone*, which is heard mostly in the speech of older people.

In other cases, an established lexical item begins to change its meaning, or take on a second meaning. The word *aggravate*, for instance, which not long ago meant exclusively 'make worse', is now often used to mean something like 'irritate', as in 'That man aggravates me'. There are some people (who write to newspaper editors) who argue that since *aggravate* is derived from the Latin *aggravare*, which has the meaning 'make worse', then that must be the true meaning of *aggravate* in English. But if this argument were applied generally, it would suggest that the real meaning of *nice*, since it is derived from the Latin *nescius*, is 'ignorant'.

There are other people who argue that giving a second meaning to *aggravate* could lead to misunderstanding. This is hardly likely, as in its first sense the verb requires an abstract object, while in its second sense it requires an animate object. For the moment, many educated people avoid using *aggravate* to mean 'irritate'. Foreign learners, while recognizing the possibility of a second meaning for *aggravate* (and for other words that are changing, as well), should probably do the same.

Stylistic variation

The choice of grammatical structure and vocabulary will vary with the situation in which people are speaking. On a formal occasion someone might say 'the person to whom I wrote', while less formally they might say 'the chap I wrote to'. One phrase is not more correct than the other. Despite the protestations of pedants, there is no reason, except custom, why words called 'prepositions' should not end sentences. What happened to be the case in Latin is not necessarily the case in English. And the word *chap* is in no way inferior to the word *person*. Likewise, swear words and slang are not wrong in themselves. Again, as with the features of pronunciation discussed earlier, it is a matter not of correctness, but of appropriateness.

When even highly educated people are chatting together with friends, their speech is very different from textbook conversations. They begin a sentence, then change their mind; they hesitate, then start again, differently; they muddle one grammatical structure with another. They omit various words, forget others, replacing them with *thingy* or *wotsit*; if necessary they will invent words just for the occasion. In a relaxed atmosphere they do not feel constrained to speak carefully, to plan what they are going to say. This makes understanding difficult for learners, of course. But once account is taken of their difficulties, when people begin to speak more carefully, inevitably the atmosphere changes somewhat.

Regional variation

Standard English, we have said, is a dialect. There are many other, regional dialects in Britain, which differ from Standard English in various ways. There are grammatical differences. So, in East Anglia the third person singular present tense is not marked with an *s*. We find *he go*, *he eat* instead of Standard English *he goes*, *he eats*. There are differences, too, of vocabulary. What is known as a *clothes horse* in Standard English and southern dialects is called a *maiden* in northern dialects.

Not everybody speaks the dialect of the area they belong to. There is a relationship between social class and dialect similar to the one between social class and accent. The higher a person's position on the social scale, the less their speech is regionally marked. This can be exemplified with the figures from a survey carried out in Norwich (which is in East Anglia). The number of third person singular present tense verb forms without *s* were counted and then expressed as a percentage of all third person singular present tense verb forms. The results for various social groups were as follows (Trudgill, 1974):

	% forms without *s*
Upper middle class	0
Lower middle class	29
Upper working class	75
Middle working class	81
Lower working class	97

In British schools great efforts are made by teachers to eradicate features of local dialect from the speech and, more particularly, the writing of their pupils. Teachers tend to think of these regional features as mistakes in Standard English. Usually they are not very successful in their efforts. It is true that the longer children stay at school, and the more successful they are, the less regionally marked, grammatically and lexically, will be their speech. But, as length of stay and success at school themselves correlate highly with social class, this may not be very significant. It is true, however, that some people do modify their speech quite considerably. In many cases they can be regarded as having two dialects, speaking Standard English in certain company and their local dialect (often with a more regional accent than they usually affect) in other company. In this way they make a claim to belong to more than one social group.

Correctness

We have mentioned the idea of correctness on a number of occasions already in this chapter. We want here just to summarize briefly what we have said. Three types of things are often said to be incorrect.

First, elements which are new to the language. Resistance to these seems inevitable, but almost as inevitable, if they prove useful, is their eventual acceptance into the language. The learner needs to recognize these and understand them. It is interesting to note that resistance seems weakest to change in pronunciation. There are linguistic reasons for this, but in addition the fact that, in RP, innovation is introduced by the social elite must play a part.

Second, features of informal speech. This, we have argued, is a matter of style, not correctness. It is like wearing clothes. There is nothing wrong, at least in our eyes, in wearing a bikini, but it is a little out of place at a dinner party (but no more than a dinner jacket would be for lying on the beach). In the same way, there are words one would not normally use when making a speech which would be perfectly acceptable in bed, and vice versa.

Third, features of regional speech. We have said little about correctness in relation to these, because we think that once they are recognized for what they are, and not thought debased forms of the prestige dialect or accent, the irrelevance of the notion of correctness will be obvious.

Summary

The most prestigious British dialect is Standard English; the most prestigious accent is RP. It is with these that learners are most familiar. What they are not usually so familiar with, however, is the degree of variation to be found within Standard English and RP. This variation, part of it stylistic, part of it attributable to changes in the language, is not the subject matter of this book (but see the section on further reading). Nevertheless, it is important that learners should be aware of its existence, and not mistake it for the social and regional variation with which we are principally concerned.

Standard English is the dialect used by educated people throughout the British Isles. Nevertheless, most people in Britain (including many who would generally be regarded as speakers of Standard English) have at least some regional dialect forms in their speech. In general, the higher people are on the social scale, the fewer of these regional forms their speech will exhibit. The main ways in which regional dialects differ from Standard English are outlined in the next chapter.

RP is not the accent of any region. It is spoken by a very small percentage of the British population, those at the top of the social scale. Everyone else has a regional accent. The lower a person is on the social scale, the more obvious their regional accent will tend to be. Differences between RP and regional accents are discussed in Chapter 4.

|2|

Dialect variation

Variation within Standard English

The Standard English dialect itself is subject to a certain amount of variation. Some of this is regional: educated people in different parts of Britain do vary to a certain extent in the way in which they speak, and even write, English. (These differences normally involve features which are also found in the regional non-standard dialects.) And some of it is to do with age: as we saw in Chapter 1, all languages and dialects change, and Standard English is no exception.

1   Speakers of Standard English in the south of England tend to use contracted negatives of the type:

> *I haven't got it*
> *She won't go*
> *Doesn't he like it?*

The further north one goes, the more likely one is to hear the alternative type:

> *I've not got it*
> *She'll not go*
> *Does he not like it?*

This is particularly true of Derbyshire, Lancashire (apart from Liverpool which, as we shall see, is in a number of ways linguistically as southern as it is northern), Cumbria and Scotland. In Scotland, forms of this type are almost invariably used. Elsewhere, it is more a matter of tendencies than of absolute rules. Southern speakers (see above) use the northern-type contraction in *I'm not*, since *I amn't* does not occur in Standard English. They also quite frequently use the *you're not*, *we're not*, *they're not* forms rather than the more typically southern-type forms with *aren't*. Part of the reason for this may lie in the stigmatized non-standard usage of this form with the first person singular, *I aren't*.

2   In most grammatical descriptions of Standard English it is stated that the indirect object precedes the direct object:

> *She gave the man a book*
> *She gave him it*
> *She gave him the book*

If the preposition *to* is employed, however, then of course the direct object can precede:

> *She gave a book to the man*
> *She gave it to him*
> *She gave a book to him*
> *She gave it to the man*

In the south of England, the forms with *to* seem to be the most common, particularly where the direct object is a pronoun. However, in the educated speech of people from the north of England, other structures are also possible, as demonstrated in the following.

(a)   *She gave it him* is very common indeed, and is also quite acceptable to many southern speakers.

(b)   *She gave it the man* is also very common in the north of England, but is not found in the south.

(c)   *She gave the book him* is not so common, but can be heard in the north of England, particularly if there is contrastive stress on *him*.

(d)   *She gave a book the man* is not especially common, but does occur in northern varieties, particularly again if *man* is contrastively stressed.

3   There are regional differences in which participle forms are used after verbs such as *need* and *want*:

Southern England:	*I want it washed*
	It needs washing
Parts of the Midlands and northern England:	*I want it washing*
	It needs washing
Scotland:	*I want it washed*
	It needs washed

4 There are a number of regional and age-group differences in the use of the verbs *must* and *have to*. These can be demonstrated with reference to table 2.1.

The forms in the (b) 'negative modal' column have the meaning 'He is not compelled to do it (but he can if he likes)' etc., while the forms in the (c) 'negative main verb' column have the meaning 'He is compelled not to do it'. The 'epistemic' uses (rows (ii) and (iv)) are those where inferences are being drawn: 'It is certain that he is in (because I can hear his radio)' etc. It can be seen that in Standard English in the south of England (the variety most often described in grammar books) only *must* appears in (c) and only *have to* or *have got to* in (b). It will also be seen that (iiic) and (vc) are blank: there is no way of saying 'He must not do it' in the past or future: one has to use constructions such as 'He wasn't allowed to do it'. In the north of England, however, these gaps are filled. At (ic), in these areas, it is possible to have *He hasn't to do it* (and, for some speakers, *He's not got to do it* or *He hasn't got to do it* – which are therefore ambiguous in a way they are not in the south of England) with the additional meaning *He mustn't do it*. Similarly, with the past, (iiic), educated northern English can have *He hadn't to do it* (as well as *He didn't have to do it* and *He hadn't got to do it* or *He'd not got to do it*, which are again ambiguous). And in the future, (vc), northern speakers have *He'll not have to do it* or *He won't have to do it* (which are ambiguous) and even *He'll haven't to do it*.

At (iic) and (ivc) the usual northern forms are *He mustn't be in* and *He mustn't have been in*. And for many younger speakers, in both the north and the south, probably as the result of North American influence, *have to* and *have got to* have also now acquired epistemic use, particularly in positive, present tense usage. Thus *He must be the greatest player in the world* can now also be *He's got to be the greatest player in the world* or *He has to be the greatest player in the world*.

5 It is possible to divide English verbs into two main classes according (among other criteria) to whether or not they employ auxiliary *do* in negatives and interrogatives:

He walked	*He didn't walk*	*Did he walk?*
He laughed	*She didn't laugh*	*Did she laugh?*
She can leave	*She can't leave*	*Can she leave?*
He will go	*He won't go*	*Will he go?*

Table 2.1 *must* and *have to* in southern English English

		(a) Positive	(b) Negative modal	(c) Negative main verb
Non-epistemic	(i)	He must do it He has to do it He's got to do it	He doesn't have to do it He hasn't got to do it	He mustn't do it
Epistemic	(ii)	He must be in		He can't be in
Non-epistemic	(iii)	He had to do it He'd got to do it	He didn't have to do it He hadn't got to do it	
Epistemic	(iv)	He must have been in		{ He couldn't have been in { He can't have been in
	(v)	He'll have to do it	He won't have to do it	

Verbs of the second type come into the category of modals and auxiliaries.

(a) The verbs *ought to* and *used to* are often described in English grammars as coming into this second category, and indeed are employed in this way by some older speakers:

He ought not to go	*Ought he to go?*
They used not to go	*Used they to go?*

With younger speakers, however – and this is particularly true of the interrogative form, especially with *used to* – these verbs are being reclassified in the first category:

He didn't ought to go	*Did he ought to go?*
They didn't use to go	*Did they use to go?*

(b) There is considerable regional and age-group variation concerning the verb *to have*. This variation concerns the extent to which *have* is treated as an auxiliary verb or as a full verb in different varieties of English.

In examining this variation, it is necessary to distinguish between stative meanings of the verb *to have* and dynamic meanings. With stative meanings, we are dealing with some kind of stable quality or state of affairs, where *to have* means something like 'to be in possession of'. With dynamic meanings, we are dealing with some kind of activity or temporary state of affairs, where the verb means something like 'to consume', 'to take', etc. Thus, *I have some coffee in the cupboard* involves stative meaning, whereas *I have coffee with my breakfast* is dynamic.

In English English, until relatively recently, the verb *to have* required *do*-support – that is, it was treated like a full verb – in the case of dynamic meanings only. Thus:

Does she have coffee with breakfast?	*No, she doesn't*
They didn't have a good time last night	

With stative meanings, on the other hand, it was treated as an auxiliary and did not require *do*-support. Thus:

Have they any money?	*No, they haven't*
They hadn't any coffee in the cupboard	

In American English, on the other hand, *do*-support is required in both cases, so the verb *to have* is treated as a main verb regardless of whether it has dynamic or stative meanings. Thus:

> *Does she have coffee with breakfast?*   *No she doesn't*
> *They didn't have a good time last night*
> *Do they have any money?*   *No, they don't*
> *They didn't have any coffee in the cupboard*

In Scottish English and, to a certain extent in the north of England as well as in many parts of Ireland, we find the opposite situation – there is no distinction between dynamic and stative meanings, but the verb *to have* is treated as an auxiliary in all cases. Thus, in addition to saying:

> *Have they any money?*   *No, they haven't*
> *They hadn't any coffee in the cupboard*

in Scottish English one can also say:

> *Has she coffee with her breakfast?*   *No, she hasn't*
> *They hadn't a good time last night*

This difference in the status of *have* is also demonstrated by different possibilities of phonological contraction (only auxiliary *have* can be contracted). Thus:

US English	*I have no money*	*I had a good time*
English English	*I've no money*	*I had a good time*
Scottish English	*I've no money*	*I'd a good time*

In both American and British English, it is also very usual with stative meanings in more informal styles to use the *have got* construction, for example:

> *Have they got any money?*   *No, they haven't*
> *They hadn't got any coffee in the cupboard*

There is also the further complcation that the American-style failure to distinguish grammatically between stative and dynamic meanings is now beginning to influence the English of England, particularly amongst younger speakers in the south of England. This means that in southern England English we now have the possibility, with stative meanings, of using three different types of construction:

> *Have you got any money?*   (informal)
> *Have you any money?*   (formal, older)
> *Do you have any money?*   (newer)

6 It is well known that certain verb-particle constructions in English have alternative forms as follows:

(a)   *He turned out the light*
      Put on your coat!
      She took off her shoes

(b)   *He turned the light out*
      Put your coat on!
      She took her shoes off

There is, however, regional variation with respect to this usage in Britain. All speakers will accept both (a) and (b) as normal English, but speakers in the south of England are more likely to employ the (b) forms in their own speech, whereas Scottish speakers almost invariably use forms of type (a).

Lexical features

We shall be dealing further with variation in vocabulary in individual sections. It is worth noting here, however, that some features such as the lack of distinction between *teach* and *learn*, and between *borrow* and *lend*, are found in nearly all non-standard dialects:

They don't learn you nothing (= They don't teach you anything)
Can I lend your bike? (= Can I borrow your bike?)

Features of colloquial style

At some points it is difficult to distinguish between features of colloquial style and those of non-standard dialect. The following are a few of these.

(a)   *us* can function as the first person singular object pronoun:

      Give us a kiss!

(b)   pronoun apposition – a personal pronoun immediately following its antecedent noun:

      My dad he told me not to

(c)   indefinite *this* – *this* can function as an indefinite article, particularly in narratives:

      There's this house, see, and there's this man with a gun

Non-standard forms

In this book we cannot provide a comprehensive list of all the grammatical differences to be found between non-standard British dialects and Standard English. We can, however, describe some of the forms most common in varieties, and point out the *type* of differences to be looked for in each area. We shall do this, briefly, in this chapter. Further examples, together with instances of lexical variation, will be cited in the individual sections of Chapter 5.

Multiple negation

There are some grammatical forms which differ from those in Standard English and which can be found in most parts of the British Isles. This is because, in these cases, it is in fact the standard dialect which has diverged from the other varieties.

A good example of this is the grammatical construction well known throughout the English-speaking world as 'the double negative'. If we take a sentence in Standard English such as

> *I had some dinner*

we can note that there are two different ways of making this sentence negative. We can either negate the verb:

> *I didn't have any dinner*

or we can negate the word *some*, by changing it to *no*:

> *I had no dinner*

These sentences do have different stylistic connotations, the latter being more formal, but they mean approximately the same thing.

The main point is that in Standard English one can perform one or other of these operations, but not both. In most other English dialects, however, one can do both these things at once. The result is 'multiple negation':

> *I didn't have no dinner*

(Linguists prefer the terms *multiple negation* or *negative concord* to the more common 'double negative' since this construction is not limited to two negatives. It is possible to have three or more: *She couldn't get none nowhere.*)

It is safe to say that constructions of the type *I didn't have no dinner* are employed by the majority of English speakers. At one time this construction was found in the standard dialect, too, and it has parallels in many other languages. It is often, however, considered to be 'wrong' by many people in the English-speaking world. This is largely because it is, like most non-standard grammatical forms, most typical of working-class speech, and for that reason tends to have low prestige. People who believe it to be 'wrong', we can say, are probably making what is ultimately a social rather than linguistic judgement.

On the other hand, there is considerable regional variation in the type of constructions in which multiple negation is permitted. The following sorts of construction occur in some non-standard dialects but not in others:

> *We haven't got only one* (= Standard English *We've only got one*)
> *He went out without no shoes on*

Other aspects of negation in non-standard dialects

The form *ain't* is not found throughout Britain, as is multiple negation, but is nevertheless extremely common. It is variously pronounced /eint/, /ɛnt/, or /int/, and has two main functions. First, it corresponds to the negative forms of the present tense of *be* in Standard English, *aren't, isn't, am not*:

> *I ain't coming*
> *It ain't there*
> *We ain't going*

Secondly, it functions as the negative present tense of auxiliary *have*, corresponding to Standard English *haven't, hasn't*:

> *I ain't done it*
> *He ain't got one*

Note, however, that it does not usually function as the negative present of the full verb *have*:

> **I ain't a clue*
> *I haven't a clue*

(The asterisk indicates an unacceptable construction.)

The form *aren't* also occurs more widely in non-standard dialects than in Standard English. In Standard English, of course, it occurs as the negation of *are* as in *we aren't, you aren't, they aren't*. It also occurs in the first person singular with the interrogative *aren't I?* But in some non-standard dialects the form *I aren't*, equivalent to Standard English *I'm not*, also occurs. (*I amn't* occurs in parts of the West Midlands and Scotland.)

Past tense of irregular verbs

Regular verbs in English have identical forms for the past tense and for the past participle, as used in the formation of perfect verb forms:

Present	Past	Present perfect
I work	I worked	I have worked
I love	I loved	I have loved

Many irregular verbs, on the other hand, have in Standard English distinct forms for the past tense and past particle:

Present	Past	Present perfect
I see	I saw	I have seen
I go	I went	I have gone
I come	I came	I have come
I write	I wrote	I have written

In many non-standard dialects, however, there is a strong tendency to bring the irregular verbs into line with the regular, the distinction being signalled only by the presence or absence of *have*. There is considerable regional variation here, but in some cases we find the original past participle used also as the past tense form:

Present	Past	Present perfect
I see	I seen	I have seen
I come	I come	I have come

(In this last case, as with *hit, put, cut* etc. in Standard English, all three forms are identical.) In other cases levelling has taken place in the other direction:

Present	Past	Present perfect
I go	I went	I have went

And in others the present tense form may be generalized:

Present	Past	Present perfect
I see	I see	I have seen
I give	I give	I have give

We can also note common forms such as:

| I write | I writ | I have writ |

and the continuation of the historical tendency to make irregular verbs regular:

| I draw | I drawed | I have drawed |

The verb *do* is also involved in social dialect variation of this type, and in a rather interesting way. As is well known to learners of English as a foreign language, *do* has two functions. It can act as a full verb, as in:

He's doing maths at school
I did lots of work

And it can also act as an auxiliary verb, and is used as such in interrogation, negation, emphasis, and 'code' (Palmer, 1974):

Did you go?
You went, did you?
We didn't go
I did like it
We went and so did they

In Standard English, the forms of the full verb and of the auxiliary are identical:

He does maths, does he?
You did lots of work, didn't you?

In most non-standard dialects, however, the full verb and the auxiliary are distinguished in the past tense, as the full verb has been subjected to the levelling process described above, while the auxiliary has not. That is, the past tense form of the full verb is *done*, that of the auxiliary *did*:

You done lots of work, didn't you?
I done it last night. Did you? Yes I did

These non-standard dialects therefore have a grammatical distinction that is not found in the standard dialect.

NEVER *as past tense negative*

In non-standard dialects in most parts of the country, the word *never*, in contrast to Standard English, can refer to a single occasion, and functions in the same way as the form *didn't*. Thus *I never done it* means 'I did not do it' with reference to a single, particular occasion. Forms of this type are particularly common in the speech of children, but are well attested in adult speech too:

> *She did yesterday, but she never today*
> *You done it! I never!*

Present tense verb forms

The present tense form of the verb in Standard English is somewhat anomalous in that the third person singular form is distinguished from the other forms by the presence of -s:

> *I want*
> *you want*
> *we want*   but   *he, she, it wants*
> *they want*

In a number of non-standard dialects, this anomaly is not found. In East Anglia (as in some American and Caribbean varieties), this verb paradigm is completely regular as a result of the absence of the third singular -s. In these dialects, forms such as the following are usual:

> *She like him*
> *It go very fast*
> *He want it*
> *He don't like it*

The individual form *don't*, in fact, is very common indeed throughout the English-speaking world in the third person singular.

In other parts of Britain, including parts of the north of England and especially the south-west and South Wales, the regularity is of the opposite kind, with -s occurring with all persons of the verb:

> *I likes it*
> *We goes home*
> *You throws it*

In parts of the west of England this leads to the complete distinction of the full verb *do* and auxiliary *do*:

	Present	Past	Past participle
Full verb:	dos	done	done
Auxiliary:	do	did	—

Thus:

> *He dos it every day, do he?*
> *He done it last night, did he?*
> (*Dos* is pronounced /duːz/.)

In other dialects, including many in Scotland and Northern Ireland, the forms with -*s* in the first and second persons and in the third person plural are a sign of the 'historic present', where the present tense is used to make the narration of past events more vivid:

> *I go home every day at four o'clock*

but

> '*I goes down this street and I sees this man hiding behind a tree . . .*'

Relative pronouns

In Standard English, *who* is used as a relative pronoun referring to human nouns, *which* for non-humans, and *that* for nouns of both types. The relative pronoun is also frequently omitted in restrictive relative clauses where it refers to the object of a verb:

That was the man who did it	*That was the man who I found*
That was the man that did it	*That was the man that I found*
	That was the man I found
That was the brick which did it	*That was the brick which I found*
That was the brick that did it	*That was the brick that I found*
	That was the brick I found

These forms are also found in non-standard dialects, but a number of additional forms also occur, including omission of pronouns referring to the subject:

> *That was the man what done it*
> *That was the man which done it*
> *That was the man as done it*
> *That was the man at done it*
> *That was the man done it*

The form with *what* is particularly common. Possessive relatives may also differ from Standard English:

> *That's the man what his son done it*

cf. Standard English   *That's the man whose son did it*

Personal pronouns

A number of interesting regional and social differences concerning the personal pronouns can be noted. These include the use in north-eastern English of *us* as a first-person singular object pronoun. This phenomenon is also commonly found in the colloquial speech of many other parts of Britain, but outside the north-east it is confined to a limited number of locutions, such as *Do us a favour* and *Give us a kiss*.

The reflexive pronouns in Standard English are formed by suffixing *-self* or *-selves* to

(a) the possessive pronoun:
    my   *myself*
    your   *yourself*
    our   *ourselves*

(b) the object pronoun:
    him   *himself*
    it   *itself*
    them   *themselves*

(The form *her* + *self herself* could be regarded as being based on either the possessive or the object pronoun.)

Many non-standard dialects have regularized this sytem so that, for instance, all forms are based on the possessives:

    myself   *herself*
    yourself   *itsself*
    hisself   *ourselves*
                      theirselves

Comparatives and superlatives

Standard English permits comparison through either the addition of *more*:

    She's more beautiful than you

or through the addition of *-er*:

    He's nicer

Many non-standard dialects permit both of these simultaneously:

    She's more rougher than he is

The same is also true with superlatives. Since Shakespeare wrote *The most unkindest cut of all* this form has been lost in Standard English, but survives in many other dialects:

He's the most roughest

Demonstratives

Corresponding to the Standard English system of:

this	*these*
that	*those*

a number of social and regional variants occur. Most commonly, Standard English *those* corresponds to *them* (sometimes, particularly in Scottish dialects, *they*) in non-standard dialects:

Look at them animals!
Look at they animals!

Adverbs

In Standard English, there are many pairs of formally related adjectives and adverbs:

He was a slow runner	*He ran slowly*
She was a very clever speaker	*She spoke very cleverly*

In most non-standard dialects, these forms are not distinct:

He ran slow
She spoke very clever
They done it very nice
cf. *He'll do it very good*

In the case of some adverbs, forms without *-ly* are also found in colloquial Standard English:

Come quick!

although some speakers might not accept this as Standard English.

Unmarked plurality

A very widespread feature indeed is that, after numerals, many nouns of measurement are not marked for plurality, in many non-standard dialects:

> *a hundred pound*
> *thirteen mile*
> *five foot*

Prepositions of place

Prepositions exhibit a large degree of variation in their usage in British dialects. This is particularly true of prepositions of place, and we can do no more here than cite a very few examples of cases where non-standard dialects can differ from Standard English:

> *It was at London (= It was in London)*
> *He went up the park (= He went to the park)*
> *I got off of the bus (= I got off the bus)*

Traditional Dialects

In most of this book, we are dealing with those accents and dialects of English in the British Isles which foreign visitors are most likely to come into contact with. In this section, however, we deal briefly with certain grammatical features associated in particular with what are often referred to as 'Traditional Dialects'.

Traditional Dialects are those conservative dialects of English which are, for the most part, spoken in relatively isolated rural areas by certain older speakers and which differ considerably from Standard English and, indeed, from one another. Traditional Dialects are what most British people think of when they hear the term *dialect* used in a non-technical way. They correspond to those varieties which are known as *patois* in the French-speaking world and *Mundart* in German-speaking areas.

Grammatical features which are typical of certain Traditional Dialects include the following:

(a) In most Scottish dialects, negation is not formed with *not*, but with *no* or with its more typically Scottish form *nae* /neǝ/. Thus we find forms in Scottish English such as:

> *He's no coming*
> *I've nae got it*
> *I cannae go*

(b) In large areas of the north of England, including urban areas of Yorkshire, as well as in many areas of the rural south-west of England, the older distinction survives between the informal singular second person pronouns *thou, thee, thine* and formal and/or plural *you, yours*. In the north of England, the usual subject and object form of this pronoun is *tha*, while in the south-east it tends to be *thee*. The system operates very much as in modern French, with friends and family being referred to as *tha* and people who one does not know so well being called *you*. It is also often the case that distinct verb forms associated with second person singular still survive; for example, *tha cast* 'you can'.

(c) In large areas of the south-west of England, including Devon and Somerset, a system of personal pronouns exists in which the form of the pronoun is not, for the most part, determined by subject versus object function but by weak or strong stress position. For example:

strong	*weak*
you	ee
he	er (subject), 'n (object)
she	er
we	us
they	'm

Thus:

> *You wouldn't do that, would ee?*
> *He wouldn't do that, would er?*
> *No, give 'n to he*
> *She wouldn't do that, would er?*
> *No, give 'n to she*
> *We wouldn't do that, would us?*
> *No, give 'n to we*
> *They wouldn't do that, would 'm?*
> *No, give 'n to they*

(d) In many Traditional Dialects of the south-west of England, the gender system operates in an interesting manner, unlike that of

Standard English, in that mass nouns such as *water* and *bread* are usually referred to as *it*, while count nouns such as *hammer* and *tree* are referred to as *he*, *er*, *'n*. Thus one would say:

> *Pass me the bread. It's on the table*

but

> *Pass me the loaf. He's on the table*

(e) In areas of the north of England and Scotland, there is a three-way distinction in the system of demonstratives, rather than the two-way system associated with Standard English. Thus, *this* and *these* refer to objects near to the speaker, *that* and *them* refer to objects near to the listener, while *yon* refers to objects remote from both parties.

(f) Forms of the verb *to be*, particularly those of the present tense, show much greater variation in Traditional Dialects than in more modern forms of speech. For example, in the north-east of England, *is* is generalized to all persons – for example, *I is*. In parts of the West Midlands, *am* may be generalized to all persons, as in *you am*, while in areas of the south-west, *be* may be generalized to all persons of the verb – that is, *you be*, *he be*, etc.

|3|

RP

In this chapter we begin by presenting a framework for the description of the sounds of English. We then outline the principal ways in which RP varies, before going on to look in detail at the sounds of RP. We do not discuss stress, rhythm, or intonation, which are beyond the scope of this book.

A framework for description

Consonants and vowels

We must begin by making a distinction between consonants and vowels. Because our interest is in pronunciation, this distinction is based on the spoken, not the written language: what we will refer to as vowels are therefore not the letters a, e i, o, u.

The first criterion for assigning sounds to the vowel category is that their production does not involve closure or sufficient narrowing of the vocal tract to cause audible friction. The second criterion is that they should typically occur in the middle of a syllable, rather than at the margins. All other sounds, including those that meet the first criterion but not the second (the first sounds of the words *run*, *lend*, *young*, *wing*) are categorized as consonants.

Describing consonants
Consonants are described in terms of the presence or absence of voicing (vibration of the vocal folds), place of articulation, and

manner of articulation. Thus the initial sound in the word *vat* is said to be a voiced labiodental fricative: the vocal folds vibrate, and the sound is created by friction of the air as it passes through a narrow gap between lip (labio-) and teeth (dental). By contrast, the initial sound in the word *fat* is a voiceless labiodental fricative (the difference being that there is no vibration of the vocal folds). And the initial sound of *sat* is a voiceless alveolar fricative (the friction takes place in the narrow gap between the tongue and the alveolar ridge). All of the consonants referred to in this book are to be found in the table on page x, which shows for each of them their place and manner of articulation, and whether or not they are voiced.

Describing vowels

A vowel can be described in terms of: the part of the tongue which is raised in producing it, and how far it is raised; and how spread or rounded the lips are. Much of this information can be captured through the use of cardinal vowel charts, which we use throughout the remainder of the book. These charts are based on the Cardinal Vowel Scale devised by Daniel Jones. This scale of sixteen vowel

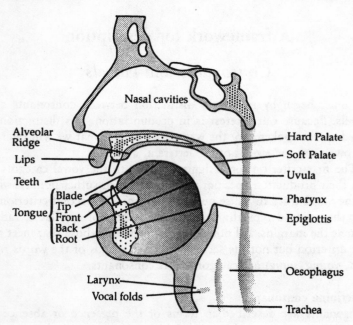

Figure 3.1 Organs of speech

sounds relates to the sounds produced when the highest part of the tongue is in eight different positions (four at the front of the mouth, four at the back), with the lips rounded, and with the lips unrounded.

The chart on page ix is a cardinal vowel chart showing the position of the sixteen cardinal vowels (as well as a number of central vowels). The chart is a schematic representation of the mouth, with 'close' referring to a position of the tongue as close to the palate as possible without friction occurring, and with 'open' referring to a position of the tongue at the bottom of the mouth. A feeling can be developed for the relationship between various positions in the vowel chart and the sounds they represent by listening to speakers reading the word list (page xi) on the cassette, while identifying the position of the vowels on the relevant vowel chart.

Phonemes and allophones

The initial sounds of the words *fan* and *vat* are clearly different. As we saw above, the first is voiceless and the second voiced. But not only are the two sounds different from each other; they also make a difference of meaning. A fan is not a van.

In RP (but not in every accent of English), the initial sound of the word *leaf* is not the same as the final sound of the word *feel*. The first is said to be 'clear', and the second (which involves the back of the tongue being drawn towards the velum) is referred to as 'dark'. In this case, however, the difference does not affect meaning. If we began the word *leaf* with a dark l rather than a clear l, we would not change its meaning. Whether we used a dark l or a clear l, we would be understood to be referring to a leaf.

All four sounds referred to in the previous two paragraphs can be represented by phonetic symbols. In order to represent sounds phonetically, we place the symbols between square brackets. We have [f] and [v], [l] (clear) and [ɫ] (dark).

Although there are four different sounds, two of them, [l] and [ɫ] are not contrastive: they do not change meaning. For this reason they may be considered as different realizations of a single linguistic unit. Such a unit is referred to as a 'phoneme' and the different realizations as 'allophones' of the phoneme.

Phonemes are represented between slants. Thus we can say that the phoneme /l/ has two allophones, [l] and [ɫ]. This allows us to give two possible transcriptions of the word *feel*, for instance. A phonemic transcription would be /fiːl/, while a more detailed, phonetic transcription would be [fiːɫ]. The usefulness of the distinction between phonemes and allophones will become apparent below.

Variability in RP

Even though we speak of RP as a single accent, there is nevertheless significant variability within it. In this section we will begin by identifying the forms that variability takes and then go on to discuss the factors that account for variability.

Forms of variability

There are three main forms of variability in RP: systemic, realizational, and lexical.

We speak of *systemic or inventory* variability when different speakers have different sets (or systems) of phonemes. In RP this applies only to vowel phonemes. Some older speakers of RP have one more vowel phoneme than others. Such speakers distinguish between pairs of words like *paw* and *pore*, pronouncing them /pɔː/ and /pɔə/ respectively. Most speakers do not have the vowel /ɔə/, and pronounce both words /pɔː/.

Realizational variability refers to the way in which a single phoneme may have different phonetic realizations. For example, all RP speakers have a phoneme /ou/ (as in *boat*), which contrasts with /ei/ (*bait*), /au/ (*bout*), and /ai/ (*bite*). They do not all pronounce it in the same way, however. Older speakers are likely to pronounce this [ou], with a back first element. The vowel phoneme of younger speakers, however, starts from a more central point, giving [bəut].

In the context of pronunciation, 'lexical' variability refers to the use of different series of phonemes for the same word. We have already noted one example in Chapter 1, the pronunciation of *economic* as /ikən'ɒmɪk/ or /ɛkən'ɒmɪk/, both of which are found amongst RP speakers. Another example is the different pronunciation of the word *off*, which may be /ɒf/ (rhyming with *cough*, and the most usual pronunciation) or /ɔːf/ (rhyming with *morph*, and usually associated with older, upper-class speakers).

All of the variability referred to above relates to individual words and to differences of pronunciation between people. In continuous speech there is further variability, some of which depends on the speed and formality of speech as much as it does on differences between people. This variability includes a number of processes: /h/ dropping (e.g. /'stopɪm/ for *stop him*; /r/ insertion e.g. /vənɪlərai skriːm/ for *vanilla ice-cream*); assimilation, as in the example in Chapter 1 of /ɪk'spɛksou/ for *expect so*. We describe conditions for /h/ dropping and /r/ insertion in the sections on these phonemes.

Factors accounting for variability

There are several factors which help to account for variability within RP. The first of these is the age of the speaker. Since RP, like any living accent, is constantly changing, there will be differences between the pronunciation of younger and older speakers. As we noted above, the old may have one more vowel phoneme than most other speakers. Younger speakers typically use more glottal stops (see below) than their elders, and use monophthongs where diphthongs have been traditional.

A second factor is social class. Members of the upper class have features which distinguish them from the majority of RP speakers. In identifying this class, Wells (1982) refers to dowager duchesses, certain army officers, Noel Coward-type sophisticates, and popular images of elderly Oxbridge dons and jolly-hockey-sticks schoolmistresses. Such speakers are likely to have, for example, a particularly open final vowel in words like *university*, close to Cardinal [ɛ].

A third factor is the age at which a person began to acquire an RP accent. Those who acquire it after childhood are likely to avoid normal features of faster RP speech, such as the dropping of unaccented /h/ in pronouns.

Other personal factors include the particular school attended; the speaker's profession or role; personality (a fastidious person may avoid something they consider vulgar, such as use of glottal stops in certain environments); attitudes to language and to other speakers of RP; the frequency with which a speaker uses a word (less frequently used words are less likely to participate in a general change of pronunciation – for example, for some speakers at least, *heir* is less likely to be monopthongized than *air*); and even what a person has been told, perhaps by a teacher, is the correct pronunciation of a word.

Other authors have concentrated on some of these factors in identifying sub-varieties of RP. For Gimson (1988) there are three main types: conservative RP, spoken by the older generation and certain professional and social groups; general RP, the least marked variety; and advanced RP, spoken by younger members of exclusive social groups. Wells (1982) also proposes three significant varieties: U-RP (upper-crust RP), spoken by the group identified as upper class above; mainstream RP, equivalent to Gimson's general RP; and adoptive RP, spoken by those who acquire the accent after childhood. In what follows, for each sound, we begin by describing mainstream RP and then identify and comment on any significant variants.

The individual sounds of RP

Consonants

We describe the consonants in sets based on their manner of articulation.

Plosives

Plosives involve three stages: the closure of the vocal tract, the compression of air, and the release of the compressed air in the form of an explosion. There are six plosive phonemes in RP:

	bilabial	alveolar	velar
voiceless	/p/	/t/	/k/
voiced	/b/	/d/	/g/

The voiceless plosives /p, t, k/ are usually marked by aspiration, a voiceless interval between release and the onset of the following sound, and so may be transcribed phonetically as [pʰ, tʰ, kʰ]. There is no aspiration, however, when the plosive follows /s/ initially in a syllable, as in /spin/. Aspiration may also be absent at the end of a word, particularly in informal speech. According to Wells (1982), stressed word-initial /p, t, k/ often have surprisingly little aspiration in the speech of upper-class speakers.

The duration of vowels (particularly long vowels) before /p, t, k/ is shorter than when they occur before /b, d, g/. Thus, for example, the vowel /iː/ in *bead* is of greater duration than when it occurs in *beat*.

The place of articulation of the alveolar plosives /t, d/ is strongly influenced by that of a following consonant. Before /θ/ (in *eighth*, for example) it will be dental; before /r/ (in *drugs*, for example) it will be post-alveolar.

The place of articulation of the velar plosives /k, g/ depends on the quality of the accompanying vowel. With /iː/, as in *leak*, the /k/ may be realized as a palatal [c]; with /ɑ:/, as in *lark*, the closure will be significantly further back.

Where two plosives occur together, either within a word or at the boundaries of words (as in *apt*, *bad boy*), the first plosive is not released. When a plosive occurs before a nasal consonant (as in *could not*), the release is nasal, that is, the air escapes through the nasal passage. When a plosive occurs before /l/ (e.g. *bottle* /bɒtl/), the release is lateral, i.e. the air escapes as a result of the raising of one or both sides of the tongue.

The glottal stop [ʔ] is a form of plosive in which the closure is made with the vocal folds, and it has long been a feature of RP, though it does not have phonemic status. It is used by some speakers to reinforce /p, t, k, č/ in a range of syllable-final environments. In such cases the glottal precedes the vowel or consonant, the process being referred to as 'glottalization' e.g. *six* [sɪʔks] = /sɪks/. The glottal stop may also mark a syllable boundary when the following syllable begins with a vowel, or stand in place of a linking or intrusive /r/ (see below).

The glottal stop is frequently used as a realization of word or morpheme final /p, t, k/ when followed by a consonant. Thus [skɒʔ lənd] for *Scotland*, [gaʔwɪk) for *Gatwick*, [geʔdaun] for *get down*. The realization of /p and k/ as [ʔ] is usually restricted to cases when the following consonant has the same place of articulation as that being realized as [ʔ]. For example: [baʔgɑ:dn̩] for *back garden*. The realization of a consonant as a glottal stop is known as 'glottalling'.

Recently there has been an extension of the use of the glottal stop as a realization of /t/ in RP. Younger speakers, upper as well as middle class, may be heard variably using a glottal stop in word-final position, either before a pause or even before a vowel. Thus [ðæʔ] for *that* and [kwaɪʔɔ:fʌl] *quite awful*. It is at least possible that the increased use of the glottal stop in RP is in part attributable to the influence of popular London speech (see Wells, 1984). Careful speakers and speakers of adoptive RP will tend to avoid glottalling.

Fricatives
Fricatives involve the making of a narrow gap which causes friction as the air passes through it. There are nine fricative phonemes in RP.

	labio-dental	dental	alveolar	palato-alveolar	glottal
voiceless	/f/	/θ/	/s/	/š/	/h/
voiced	/v/	/ð/	/z/	/ž/	

The voiced fricatives /v, ð, z, ž/ are only partially voiced (or may be not voiced at all) when they occur finally. They may be distinguished from their voiceless counterparts, however, by the greater duration of the vowel which precedes them. For instance, the vowel /i:/ will have greater duration in *freeze* than in *fleece*.

The palato-alveolar fricative /ž/ occurs only medially (as in *measure*), except in French loan words such as *genre* and *prestige*.

The glottal fricative /h/ only occurs in syllable initial positions immediately preceding a vowel. The phonetic realization of /h/ depends on the quality of the vowel it precedes, since the sound is produced through the voiceless expulsion of air from the lungs with the mouth and tongue already in position for the following vowel. The sound of /h/ in *heat* is quite different from that in *heart*, for example.

As noted above, /h/ is usually dropped when it occurs in unstressed pronouns (*he, him, her, his*) and auxiliaries (*has, have, had*). Thus [stɒpɪm] for *stop him*. Careful speakers and speakers of adoptive RP are less likely to drop /h/, probably having been influenced by the stigma attached to more general h-dropping in other accents (see below).

Affricates
An affricate is a plosive with a sufficiently slow release for friction to occur during that stage. In our analysis there are just two affricate phonemes: /č/ and /ĵ/, palato-alveolar, voiceless and voiced respectively.

Nasals
Nasal consonants involve a closure within the mouth, but with the velum lowered so that air can escape through the nose. There are three nasal phonemes in RP: bilabial /m/, alveolar /n/, and velar /ŋ/. They are voiced, though there may be partial devoicing when they follow a voiceless consonant. All three nasals, but most commonly /n/, may be syllabic. Thus *button* may be /bʌtn̩/.

The bilabial nasal /m/ and the alveolar nasal /n/ are normally realized as the labiodental [ɱ] before /f/ and /v/. Thus *comfort* will be [kʌɱfət] and *invoice* [iɱvɔis]. Before /θ/ and /ð/, as in *tenth*, /n/ may be dental [n̪]; before /r/, as in *unready*, it may be post-alveolar.

Older upper-class speakers may have /in/ (rather than the usual /ɪŋ/) for the verbal ending *-ing*. So, /fišin/ for *fishing*. As the restricted age of those who display it implies, this feature seems to be in decline.

The velar nasal does not occur word initially.

Lateral /l/

Laterals involve the continuous escape of air through one or both sides of the mouth. There is only one lateral phoneme in RP, which is normally voiced and which has three allophones. Two of these have been referred to above: clear [l], which is found before vowels and /j/; and dark [ɫ], which is found after a vowel, before a consonant, and syllabically e.g. [bɒtɫ] for *bottle*. The third allophone is voiceless [l̥], which is most noticeable after aspirated /p/ and /k/, as in *plate* and *clap*.

Some RP speakers use a vowel in place of dark [ɫ] in certain environments. Gimson (1988) includes *table* ['teibö] and *beautiful* as examples, making reference to preceding labial articulations. The apparent increase in the vocalization of /l/ in RP may be coming about under the influence of popular London speech, where it is to be found more frequently and in a wider range of environments (see Chapter 5). The authors know one elderly RP speaker, brought up in a solid middle-class home in Hampstead, who has always said [mɪök] for *milk*.

Post-alveolar approximant /r/

The phoneme /r/ occurs only before a vowel. It has a number of allophones. The most common is a voiced post-alveolar frictionless approximant [ɹ]. Following /d/ it is fricative. Following stressed /p, t, k/ it is typically devoiced [ɹ̥]. Between vowels, when the first vowel is stressed, and following a dental fricative /r/ may be realized by the tip of the tongue tapping the alveolar ridge [ɾ] (alveolar tap). According to Wells (1982), this tapped [ɾ] is typical of some varieties of upper-class RP.

When words which once ended in /r/ (indicated by the spelling) are followed by a word beginning with a vowel, what is called a linking /r/ is normally introduced. Thus: /fɑ:/ *far*, but /fɑ:rəwei/ *far away*.

Even when there is no historical /r/, if a word ends with a non-high vowel and precedes a word beginning with a vowel, again an /r/ may be inserted. Thus /kænədəriz/ *Canada is*. Although in cases like this the /r/ is referred to as 'intrusive', the phenomenon is very much a part of RP. Careful speakers and speakers of adoptive RP may, however, avoid it (possibly introducing a glottal stop between the words, as noted above). Some speakers may even avoid the use of linking /r/. Though still stigmatized, there is some tendency, as in many non-RP accents, for intrusive /r/ to occur within words before a suffix, e.g. /drɔ:riŋ/ for *drawing*.

Semi-vowels

There are two semi-vowel phonemes in English: /w/ and /j/. As noted earlier, though semi-vowels are vowel-like, they are treated as consonants because they function more like consonants.

The labio-velar semi-vowel /w/ is articulated with the tongue in a back half-close position and with lip rounding. It is normally voiced, but following accented /t/ or /k/ it is completely devoiced [ʍ]. Consonants immediately preceding /w/ typically show lip rounding in anticipation.

Some RP speakers omit /w/ in some words that begin /kw/ for other speakers. Thus /kɔ:tə/ for *quarter*.

The palatal semi-vowel /j/ is articulated with the tongue in a front half-close to close position. There may be lip rounding in anticipation of a following vowel which has lip rounding. It is normally voiced, but after accented /p, t, k, h/ (as in *cuter*) there is complete devoicing and /j/ is realized as a palatal fricative [ç].

There is lexical variation relating to the presence or absence of /j/ after /s/ and /l/ in such words as *suit* and *lute*: /su:t/~/sju:t/. The absence of /j/ is increasingly common.

There is a tendency for /j/ to coalesce with preceding alveolar plosives to form affricates, particularly in informal speech. By this process [tj] becomes [č] and [dj] becomes [j]. This occurs when a word ending in /t, d/ precedes *you* or *your*, e.g. [wɒčuni:d] *what you need*, or [wuǰʊ] *would you*.

Within words, this j-coalescence is found most often where the second syllable involved is unstressed, e.g. *soldier* [soulǰə]. Within a stressed syllable, such as *tune* [ču:n], coalescence may not be recognized as RP, though it does occur in the speech of RP speakers.

Careful speakers will tend to avoid j-coalescence.

Vowels

MONOPHTHONGS

In our analysis of RP there are twelve monophthongs, that is, relatively pure vowels. Typical realizations for these are shown in figure 3.2. We shall treat each of them in turn.

/i:/ as in *bee*.

The lips are spread.

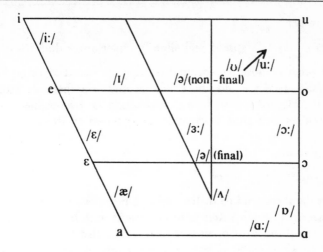

Figure 3.2 Typical realizations of RP monophthongs

The vowel usually involves a glide from the position indicated for /ɪ/ in figure 3.2 to that for /iː/. Pronunciation of this vowel without a glide is perceived as affected.

There is a growing tendency for the final vowel in words like *city* and *pity* to have a vowel rather more like /iː/ than the traditional /ɪ/. Thus /sɪtiː/ rather than the older /sɪtɪ/. The plurals and possessive forms of such words, however, have /ɪ/. Thus /sɪtɪz/ for *cities* or *city's*.

/ɪ/ as in *pit*

The lips are loosely spread.

Older speakers tend to have a closer vowel than do the young. However, many older upper-class speakers have a strikingly open final vowel in words like *city* [sɪtɛ̀].

There is a tendency for traditional /ɪ/ to be replaced by /ə/ in some unstressed syllables. In general, younger people are more likely to have /ə/, upper-class speakers are more likely to have /ɪ/. Environments for this lexical variability are: the first vowel of the endings -*ity* (*possibility*), -*itive* (*positive*), -*ily* (*merrily*), -*ate* (*fortunate*), -*ible* (*visible*), -*em* (*problem*); other unstressed syllables -*ess* (*hopeless*), -*ace* (*furnace*), -*age* (*manage*), -*et* (*bracelet*), *be-* (*believe*). The ratio of /ɪ/ to /ə/, which varies not only between the different environments listed above but also within them, is too complex to report here.

/ɛ/ as in *pet*

The lips are loosely spread and slightly wider apart than for /ɪ/.

An /ɛ/ which is close to Cardinal [e] may be heard amongst older upper-class speakers and those who would use them as models. Gimson (1988) says that such a realization is 'over-refined' while one which forms a glide towards [ə] is perceived as affected.

/æ/ as in *pat*

The lips are neutrally open.

Younger speakers tend to realize /æ/ as a more open vowel, which in some cases may cause listeners to confuse it with /ʌ/. The tendency for /æ/ to become more open over time is true also for /ɪ/ and /ɛ/, the changes to all three being part of one process. As with /ɛ/, a closer realization of /æ/, around Cardinal [ɛ], or with a glide towards [ə] may be perceived as refined.

There is lexical variability involving /æ/ and /ɑː/, both being used in the following words, amongst others: *plastic, plasticine, lather, photograph, elastic, transfer.*

/ʌ/ as in *putt*

The lips are neutrally open.

Older speakers typically realize /ʌ/ as a rather more retracted vowel than that indicated in figure 3.2.

/ɑː/ as in *bard*

The lips are neutrally open.

Upper-class speakers may have a more retracted realization, close to Cardinal [ɑ].
Note the lexical variability between /ɑː/ and /æ/ referred to above.

/ɒ/ as in *pot*

There is slight open lip-rounding.

There is lexical variability between /ɒ/ and /ɔː/ in words where the vowel precedes /f/ /s/ /θ/ as in *off, cross, across, soft, cloth.* Many older, particularly upper-class, speakers favour /ɔː/. Younger upper-class speakers may have /ɒ/ in at least some of these words.

In words which have *al* or *au* in the spelling, there is also variation between /ɒ/ and /ɔː/, e.g. *salt, fault, Austria*.

/ɔː/ as in *board*

There is medium lip rounding.

The great majority of RP speakers use this vowel in words that once were pronounced with [ɔə] (e.g. *court, four, door*). They therefore make no distinction between, for example, *caught* and *court* [kɔːt]. Some older speakers maintain the distinction, and so have an extra vowel phoneme /ɔə/. This represents a clear case of systemic variability.

There are a growing number of RP speakers who also use /ɔː/ in at least some words in which /ʊə/ has been traditional: for example, *cure, tour, poor, sure*. For the moment this has to be seen as a case of lexical variability, but the existence of speakers for whom almost every potential /ʊə/ word is pronounced with /ɔː/ suggests that /ʊə/ may eventually lose its phonemic status. The relatively infrequent words *dour* and *lure* appear to be the only words pronounced with /ʊə/ by at least one speaker known to the authors.

/ʊ/ as in *put*

The lips are closely rounded.

There is lexical variability between /ʊ/ and /uː/ in a number of words, including *room* (a single speaker may have /uː/ in *room* but /ʊ/ in *bathroom*), *groom, broom* and *tooth*.

/uː/ as in *boot*

The lips are closely rounded.

There is growing centralization of this vowel. In upper-class RP, centralization is restricted to its occurrence immediately following /j/.

/ɜː/ as in *bird*.

There is no lip rounding.

This vowel varies between half open and half close.

/ə/ as in *father* (final vowel)

There is no lip rounding.

Referred to as 'schwa', this vowel is never stressed. In final position, as in *carer*, it is usually more open than elsewhere, as in *regret*, for example.

DIPHTHONGS

There are eight diphthongs in our analysis of RP. Three of these are centring, that is, having schwa /ə/ as the second element. The other five diphthongs are closing, with the first element in each being more open than the second.

Centring diphthongs

See figure 3.3 for typical realizations.

/ɪə/ as in *beer*

There is no lip rounding.

Associated with upper-class RP (but often perceived as affected) is a second element which is more open.

/ɛə/ as in *bear*

There is no lip rounding.

There is variability between [ɛə] and [ɛː], with the monophthong

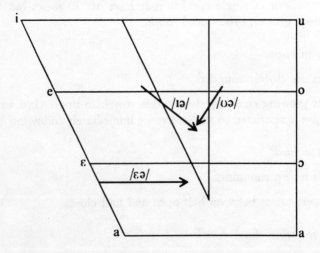

Figure 3.3 Typical realizations of RP centring diphthongs

being favoured by younger speakers, and [ɛə] being perhaps more common in less frequently occurring words in their speech. Thus for a single speaker, *air* may most often be [ɛ:] and *heir* [ɛə].

/uə/ as in *poor*

There is some initial lip rounding.

As noted above, many speakers have /ɔ:/ in words that were traditionally pronounced with /uə/.

Closing diphthongs

See figure 3.4 for typical realizations.

/ei/ as in *bay*

The lips are spread.

The starting point varies between half closed (old fashioned) and half open.

/ai/ as in *buy*

The lips are somewhat spread for the second element.

As with /ei/ there is variation in the openness of the first element, individual speakers keeping them far enough apart to maintain a distinction.

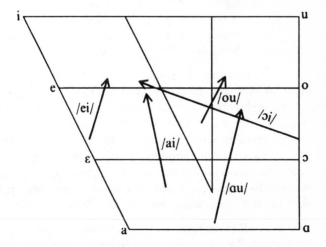

Figure 3.4 Typical realizations of RP closing diphthongs

/ɔi/ as in *boy*

The lips are rounded for the first element.

/ou/ as in *boat*

The lips are somewhat rounded for the second element.

The first element is usually [ə], a more fronted realization being regarded as affected. Older speakers may have [o] as the first element, as do some younger speakers when the vowel precedes [ɫ].

/ɑu/ as in *bout*

The lips may be somewhat rounded for the second element.

Some upper-class speakers have a fronted second element [ʉ], which may cause listeners to confuse the vowel with /ai/. Thus one person's *house* may appear to rhyme with another speaker's *mice*.

Closing diphthongs followed by schwa /ə/
All five closing diphthongs may be followed by /ə/ within a word, either as an integral part of the word (e.g., *hire*, /haiə/) or as a suffix, e.g., *higher* /haiə/).

While all three vowel elements may be maintained in careful or slow speech, in faster speech the second element is usually omitted. Examples of this process, known as 'smoothing', are:

tyre	/taiə/	>	[taə]
tower	/tɑuə/	>	[tɑə]
layer	/leiə/	>	[leə]
slower	/slouə/	>	[sloə]

[aə] and [ɑə]: The notional difference in the first element of the reduced forms of *tyre* and *tower* is so small that the two words (and others like them) have become homophones for many speakers. This reduction of two distinctive sounds into one is referred to as 'levelling'. Some younger speakers carry it further by reducing the diphthongal [ɑə] to a long monophthong [ɑː], with the result that, for them, *tyre*, *tower*, and *tar* are homophones. Monophthongization of this kind seems to be less likely when the schwa represents a suffix. Thus *fire* may become [fɑː], while *flyer* remains [flaə].

[eə]: This may be levelled with /ɛə/, so that *layer* and *lair* for example, may be homophones. Both may be further reduced to [ɛː] (see above), though there is resistance to monophthongization where the schwa represents a suffix. Thus *layer*, meaning 'stratum', is more likely to be realized as [lɛ:] than is *layer* meaning 'something or someone who lays'.

[oə]: The reduced form of /ouə/ may be realized as [ə:], levelling with /ɜ:/. Thus *slower* and *slur* may be homophones.

The recordings

The reader of the word list is relatively young and therefore has (WL15 bear /bɛ:/ and (WL42) poor /pɔ:/. There are three other speakers, two men aged about forty and a woman who is about thirty. All have been to public school. The first and third speakers would generally be regarded as mainstream RP speakers. The second speaker, however, may be regarded as a marginal RP speaker, since there are features of his speech which might cause other RP speakers to think of him as a near-RP speaker from the south-east of England.

Differences between the speakers.

1. There is no apparent systemic variability between the speakers.

2. There is some lexical variability between them:

(a) Speaker 1 has /i:/ and /ɪ/ variably as the final vowel in words like *city* [compare *unfriendly* (line 6) with *seedy* (line 14)]. In this he is more conservative than the other two speakers, who have /i:/ throughout.

(b) In the word *if*, Speaker 1 has /v/ (line 3) rather than the more common /f/ (Speaker 3), line 14).

(c) Speaker 1 has /ɒ/ as the first vowel in *contrasted* (line 34). This would usually be an indication of a north of England background, which the speaker does not have. It may be related to carefulness of speech.

3. Realizational variability.

(a) Speaker 2 realizes /ai/ with a more retracted initial element than the others.

(b) While all three speakers have a fronted realization of /u:/ (unlike more conservative speakers), Speaker 3 also exhibits very little lip rounding, at least some of the time.

(c) Speaker 2 exhibits more glottalization than the others. This feature and his realization of /ai/ (see 3 (a) above) will contribute to some RP speakers possibly considering him to be a near-RP speaker.

(d) Speaker 1 releases plosives in environments in which most speakers would not (e.g. *tacked down* (line 35). This feature is a marker of careful speech.

(e) Speaker 1 has a noticeably open and back realization of final /ə/ (e.g. *gear*, line 3).

(f) Speaker 3 has a more fronted first element in /ou/.

It is also worth noting the occasional presence of what is called 'creaky voice' in the speech of Speaker 3 (e.g. *very thick*, line 39), which is a not uncommon feature in RP.

Speaker 1

The first speaker talks about the advantages and disadvantages of living in Milton Keynes, where he lives and works.

The advantages are that you don't need a car. There's quite good shopping. It's been landscaped absolutely superbly, with beautiful roads. And if you live in any of the houses, you don't know the roads are there, just because of the way they've built them. Erm, it's new,
5 and it's clean, erm . . . Some of the disadvantages are that the people are horrible and unfriendly erm . . . They're brusque and ill-educated nouveau riche erm . . . thugs basically. . . rich, thick thugs . . . erm . . . who make life really miserable . . . erm . . . on things like the roads; there are a lot of belly-aching and V-signs and insults . . . erm
10 . . . There's quite a lot of unemployment. Certainly, five years ago it had the highest suicide rate of any city in Britain. I don't know whether that's still true. And it's now old enough for bits of it to be falling apart. And the bits that are falling apart are doing so in a horrible and really seedy, ugly way. So there's a lot of, er, depressed
15 and unhappy and very poor people there as well. So you've got erm . . . it's a kind of reflection of the nation. You've got rich with no worries at all, and deeply poor and ground down.

[The speaker goes on to talk about being burgled twice]

20 The first time, I got home, I got off my bike, and everything, and was actually undoing the front door, and looked at the window, thought God, I'm sure I didn't leave – the venetian blind, it was all crooked and bent – I can't have left it like that, and I'd actually got the door

25 unlocked before I even realized what it was that had occurred, and I
went in and there was very little mess, and gradually I noticed what
was missing – the video recorder immediately, but during the course
of the evening I kept finding more things that were no longer there –
erm, there were only four things altogether, I think a video, a Sony
Walkman, erm, and a couple of other things which I can't remember.
30 But the second occasion was much worse, er it was a hell of a mess,
erm with upturned gear, er all the covers opened and the stuff pulled
out, erm even in the kitchen where the stuff is very boring . . . erm
. . . and everything that had any value at all seemed to me to have
been taken . . . and very carefully, which contrasted with the mess
35 . . . the hi-fi had all its cabling neatly tacked down, running around
the skirting boards. It'd been pulled up incredibly neatly. So not only
did they take the gear but also all the cabling as well. Er . . . and so
far . . . erm . . . the dealings with the insurance company have been
fraught with sort of misunderstanding and erm lack of progress.

Note: *V-sign* (line 9) is a rude gesture made with two fingers.

Speaker 2

The second speaker describes a motoring accident in which he was
involved.

I'll tell you a s . . . a story about something that . . . that happened a
couple of years ago erm . . . I was driving in . . . driving in to work
one day . . . and er it was a . . . a fairly normal day . . . th . . . the
road was a little bit wet, and other than that there was good visibility
5 . . . and I was coming . . . er . . . in along one of the . . . one of the
access roads to the er university, when er a car, a Ford Capri, came
towards me, and . . . erm . . . I realized that this car was about to hit
me . . . erm . . . so I . . . I braked quite hard and er . . . erm . . .
stopped. The car hit me quite hard on the . . . on the right hand side
10 . . . and . . . erm . . . my immediate reaction was to make sure that er
the . . . the driver of the other car realized that he . . . that he was in
the . . . in the wrong. So I rolled down my window and said to him
. . . erm . . . What . . . what the heck do you think you're doing?
You've . . . you've er made a mess of my car. And the . . . the driver,
15 who was a young man, apologized and said yes . . . erm . . . his . . .
his his brakes erm locked and he . . . and he skidded on the . . . on
the wet surface. Erm, anyway, it er subsequently transpired that this

. . . this young man in fact worked for a . . . a . . . a company that repairs cars . . . erm . . . it . . . he'd . . . he'd come to the university to collect it . . . er the reason has that erm the car was going in to have its brakes fixed . . .   erm . . .   so it wasn't surprising perhaps
20 that the brakes locked. It subsequently transpired that the . . . the easiest way of er transporting my car, which was . . . which couldn't be driven away, was for this young man to phone his . . . his own company and get the . . . the erm . . . lorry out that erm . . . to get the salvage lorry out. So this . . . this happened . . . the salvage lorry
25 came round, and the erm . . . er . . . my car was then taken off to the garage . . . and erm . . . I then thought about it, and talked to my insurance company. . . er . . . they said yes, it was all right for them to do the repair . . . erm . . . and which they subsequently did . . . I . . . I reckoned that to be quite a good idea to get them to do the
30 repair since . . . since they made the . . . made the mess in the first place, I was quite likely to have quite a good repair done. And so it was . . . and erm . . . and in fact I then decided to use the same company to service my car . . . and the er . . . the man in the erm . . . the . . . the owner of the . . . of the garage said: 'Well this isn't the
35 usual way we get customers'.

Speaker 3

The third speaker is a thirty year old woman. She describes a visit to the Amazon which she made some years previously.

Um . . . in the days before husbands and children, um I did quite a lot of travelling and um . . . one of the th . . . places I went to was to the Amazon and um I hadn't really as why I . . . I knew my husband and um . . . then but . . . just as a friend really and so we um decided
5 that we, or he decided that we would go to Brazil and er I'd been travelling anyway. . . came back for Christmas, two days to wash my rucksack and off we went to Rio . . . and um I hadn't given it any thought at all and the next thing I knew we went up to Manaus, which is a free port up on the Amazon where we met some chap
10 who'd got a boat um which was rather like the *African Queen* um . . . and I felt like Katharine Hepburn . . . and we then um went in this boat up the Amazon and then off up one of the tributaries . . . um where we then came across this little South American tribe, some

Indians um who lent us a canoe . . . so we then left most of our
15   luggage behind and just took a rucksack with a cu . . . with a T-shirt
and a toothbrush and a bag of rice and a rifle . . . and then we had a
hammock and a mosquito net, which didn't bode well and . . . off we
went um . . . then w . . . on foot . . . er it was very wet and er oh we
just we and the vegetation was very thick and we . . . we had to . . .
20   we had a guide and a cook and a . . . and another boy . . . and um
. . . so we went off in our . . . in our canoes and then . . . left those in
the side in some reeds somewhere and then walked . . . um . . . we
walked for four days into the jungle . . . um . . . the mosquitoes were
appalling, the rain was appalling . . . um and we were hungry and i
25   . . . in four days it was just very interesting that you could feel
yourself reverting back to nature . . . well if . . . yes I mean there
. . . when we first got into the i . . . o . . . actually sort of out of the
canoe and into the jungle . . . um our guide had er [terrible?] . . . had
bare feet and he . . . d . . . I mean he didn't speak any, any English at
30   all but um . . . suddenly you could see that he just leaped and . . .
and you c . . . see the whites of his eyes and he'd trodden on a deadly
poisonous snake . . . something called a siracucu . . . and he'd've
been dead in thirty seconds if it'd bitten him . . . um and without
him I mean he was our guide and without him we would never have
35   got out again . . . um so that was quite dangerous and . . . I mean
who knows what sort of . . . animals were . . . or . . . or reptiles were
around at night and all spiders or whatever . . . monkeys yuh, yuh
and turtles and . . . but you know the vegetation was so . . . it was so
thick that . . . I mean . . . you couldn't see . . . I don't know te . . . er
40   . . . ten feet in front of you . . . and so we we literally had machetes
and we we were cutting our way through the . . . through the under-
growth . . . but the flora and fauna were s . . . I mean it was just
beautiful . . . um . . . no it was a very it was a . . . an incredible
experience really because it's very unusual in your lives that you're
45   . . . or . . . in this civilization that we live in . . . um that . . . that you
ever go without and that you actually are concerned for your . . . for
your welfare or and . . . that you wonder where your next meal's
going to come from.

4

Regional accent variation

As we have already seen, the accent of British English which has been most fully described, and which is usually taught to foreign learners, is the accent known as RP.

In this chapter we shall, first, give a brief outline of the main regional differences to be found in non-RP accents of British English and compare them with RP. We do not attempt to give a detailed account of all the regional and social differences in pronunciation to be found in British Isles English. In particular, we do not attempt at all to describe accents associated with Traditional Dialects, spoken by older people in rural areas (for these, see Wakelin, 1972). Rather we concentrate on urban and other regional accents of the type which are most widely heard as one travels round the country, and which are most likely to be encountered by foreign visitors. More detailed discussion of phonological features takes place in Chapter 5. Intonational and other prosodic features are not dealt with, but can of course be noted from the tape.

Regional accent differences

1 The vowel /ʌ/
(a) One of the best known differences between English accents is one of phoneme inventory – the presence or absence of particular phonemes (see p. 36). Typically, the vowel /ʌ/ does not occur in the accents of the north and Midlands of England, where /ʊ/ is to be found in those words that elsewhere have /ʌ/. The vowel /ʌ/ is

relatively recent, in the history of English, having developed out of /ʊ/, and northern accents have not taken part in this development. The result is that pairs of words such as *put: putt, could: cud* which are distinguished in Welsh, Scottish, Irish and southern English accents are not distinguished in the north and Midlands, where words like *blood* and *good, mud* and *hood*, are perfect rhymes. (There are a few common words, though, which have /ʌ/ in the south of England but which have /ɒ/ in much of the north of England. These include *one*, which rhymes with *on* in these areas, *tongue*, and *none*.)

Many northern speakers, under the influence of RP, have a vowel which is between /ʊ/ and /ʌ/ in quality in words such as *but* (and sometimes in words such as *put* also). Generally, this vowel is around [ə] (see table 4.1). This is particularly true of younger, middle-class speakers in areas of the southern Midlands. (Some speakers too, of course, hypercorrect – see Chapter 1.)

We can also note that many (particularly older) northern speakers, while they do not have /ʌ/, do have /uː/ rather than /ʊ/ in words such as *hook, book, look, took, cook*. They therefore distinguish pairs such as *book* and *buck*, which in the south are distinguished as /bʊk/ and /bʌk/, as /buːk/ and /bʊk/. (All English English accents have shortened the original long /uː/ in *oo* words to /ʊ/ in items such as *good, hood*; and all seem to have retained /uː/ in words such as *mood, food*. But in other cases there is much variation. RP speakers may have either /uː/ or /ʊ/ in *room, broom*; eastern accents have /ʊ/ rather than /uː/ in *roof, hoof*: western accents, as well as those from parts of Wales, may have /ʊ/ rather than /uː/ in *tooth*; and so on.)

(b) It is usual, in decriptions of RP, to consider /ʌ/ and /ə/ as distinct vowels, as in *butter* /bˈʌtə/). This also holds good for accents of the south-east of England, Ireland, and Scotland. However, speakers from many parts of Wales, western England, and the Midlands (as well as some northern speakers – see above) have vowels that are identical in both cases: *butter* /bˈətə/, *another* /ənˈəðə/ (see table 4.1).

Table 4.1   /ʌ/, /ʊ/ and /ə/

	but	put
RP	/ʌ/	/ʊ/
Northern	/ʊ/	/ʊ/
Western; modified northern I	/ə/	/ʊ/
Modified northern II	/ə/	/ə/
Hypercorrect northern	/ʌ/	/ʌ/

2 /æ/ and /ɑː/

Another very well known feature which distinguishes northern from southern English accents concerns the vowels /æ/ and /ɑː/. In discussing this feature we have to isolate a number of different classes of words:

(i)	*pat, bad, cap*	RP /pæt/ etc.
(ii)	*path, laugh, grass*	RP /pɑːθ/ etc.
(iii)	*dance, grant, demand*	RP /dɑːns/ etc.
(iv)	*part, bar, cart*	RP /pɑːt/ etc.
(v)	*half, palm, banana, can't*	RP /hɑːf/ etc.

RP has /æ/ in set (i), and /ɑː/ in all other sets. This incidence of vowels in the different sets is also found in all south-eastern English and in many southern Irish accents. In the Midlands and north of England, on the other hand, words in sets (ii) and (iii) have the vowel /æ/ rather than /ɑː/, although they do have /ɑː/ in the classes of (iv) and (v). Thus, whereas southerners say /grɑːs/ *grass*, /grɑːnt/ *grant*, northerners say /græs/ and /grænt/. (Normally /æ/ is pronounced [a] in most northern areas.)

This difference between the north and south of England is due to the fact that the original short vowel /æ/ was lengthened in the south of England (a) before the voiceless fricatives /f/, /θ/, /s/; and (b) before certain consonant clusters containing an initial /n/ or /m/. Change (a) affected most words in southern English accents. Exceptions include words such as: *daffodil, gaff, Jaffa, raffle, Catherine, maths, ass, crass, gas, hassle, lass, mass, chassis, tassel*, which have /æ/ in RP and southern accents. There are also some words which vary: some southerners have /æ/ in *graph, photograph, alas*, others have /ɑː/.

Change (b) is rather more complex and less complete. We can note the following phonological contexts, and typical southern English pronunciations:

	/ɑː/		/æ/
– nt	*plant*	but	*pant*
– ns	*dance*	but	*romance*
– nš†	*branch*	but	*mansion*
– nd	*demand*	but	*band*
– mp	*example*	but	*camp*

†Many speakers actually have [č] rather than [š] here
(Words such as *transport, plastic* can have either /æ/ or /ɑː/.)

Some Welsh and Irish accents (like many Australian accents) have change (a) but not change (b): they have /grɑːs/ *grass* but /dæns/ *dance*.

This discussion of the incidence of /æ/ and /ɑː/ in words like *grass* and *dance* is not relevant to Scottish and northern Irish accents (except for some RP influenced accents – some middle-class Edinburgh speakers, for example). These accents do not have the vowel /ɑː/, and therefore have /æ/ not only in sets (i), (ii) and (iii), but also in sets (iv) and (v). (The /æ/ may be pronounced [æ], [a] or [ɑ] in these varieties.) They do not, that is, have any contrast between pairs such as *palm*: *Pam*, *calm*: *cam*.

This is also true of those accents most typical of the south-west of England (see figure 4.1). RP speakers in this area do, of course, have the /æ/: /ɑː/ contrast, as do many other middle-class speakers whose accents resemble RP. But speakers with more strongly regional south-western accents do not have the contrast, or at most have a contrast that is variable or doubtful. It is certain that south-western accented speakers have /æ/ (often pronounced [a·]) in words of classes (i), (ii) and (iii). (For class (4) see below.) The doubt lies in what these speakers do with words of set (v). Typically, it seems, words such as *father*, *half*, *can't* have /æ/. Words such as *palm*, *calm* retain the /l/, and generally have /ɑ/: /pɑlm/. More recent loan words like *banana*, *gala*, *tomato*, which have /ɑː/ in south-eastern and northern English accents and /æ/ in Northern Ireland and Scotland, most typically have /æ/ but *may* have /ɑː/, and are even pronounced [təmˈɑːɹtou] etc. by some western speakers.

3 /ɪ/ and /iː/

Another major north/south differentiating feature involves the final vowel of words like *city, money, coffee* (as well as unstressed forms of *me, he, we*). In the north of England these items have /ɪ/:/sˈɪtɪ/*city.* In the south of England, on the other hand, these words have /iː/:/sˈɪtiː/. The dividing line between north and south is in this case a good deal further north than in the case of the previous two features, only Cheshire, Lancashire and Yorkshire and areas to the north being involved – except that, again, Liverpool is in this case southern rather than northern. Tyneside and Humberside too, have /iː/ rather than /ɪ/.

Scottish accents typically have the same vowel in this final position as they have in words such as *gate, face*: e.g. *hazy* [hˈeze] while southern Ireland has /iː/.

A = /æ/ in *path*
B = /ɑ:/ in *path*
C = /æ/-/ɑ:/ contrast absent or in doubt

Figure 4.1

4 /r/

Most English accents permit /r/ where it occurs *before* a vowel, as in
rat, *trap*, *carry*. They vary, however, in whether they permit the
pronunciation of /r/ after a vowel ('post-vocalic' /r/), as in words
such as *bar* and *bark*. RP does not have post-vocalic /r/ and has *bar*
/bɑ:/, *bark* /bɑ:k/. Scottish and Irish accents (like most North American accents) do have /r/ in this position.

Within England and Wales the position of post-vocalic /r/ in regional accents is quite complex, but we can generalize and say that the pronunciation with /r/ is being lost – post-vocalic /r/ is dying out – and that one is more likely to hear post-vocalic /r/s in the speech of older, working-class rural speakers than from younger middle-class urban speakers. Figure 4.2 shows those areas where post-vocalic /r/ still occurs in urban speech.

This difference between English accents is due to a linguistic change involving the loss of post-vocalic /r/, which began some

A = post-vocalic /r/ present
B = post-vocalic /r/ absent

Figure 4.2

centuries ago in the south-east of England, and has since spread to other regions. This loss of /r/ has also had a further consequence (see also p. 41). The consonant /r/ was lost, in these accents, before a following consonant, as in *cart*, but *not* before a following vowel, as in *carry*. This meant that whether or not the /r/ was pronounced in words like *car* depended on whether it was followed by a word beginning with a vowel or a word beginning with a consonant (or by a pause). Thus we have:

	car engine	with /r/	/kɑːrˈɛnjɪn/
but	*car port*	without /r/	/kɑː pɔːt/

The /r/ in the pronunciation of *car engine* is known as 'linking r'. Originally, we can assume, what happened was that you *deleted* (or failed to pronounce) the /r/ before a following *consonant*. Subsequently, however, this pattern has been restructured, analogically, for most speakers, so that it is now interpreted in such a way that you *insert* an r before a following *vowel*. This means that analogous to:

> *soar* /sɔː/   *soar up* /sɔːr ʌp/

we now also have:

> *draw* /drɔː/   *draw up* /drɔːr ʌp/

Where r occurs in this position – where there is no r in the spelling (the spelling reflects the original pronunciation, of course) – it is known as 'intrusive r'. Because there is no r in the spelling, intrusive /r/ has often been frowned upon by school teachers and others as being 'incorrect'. However, it is now quite normal in those accents of English which are 'r-less', and even in RP it is quite usual for speakers to say:

> *idea of*   *Shah of Persia*
> *draw it*   *India and*

and other such phrases with an /r/. We can say that where one of the vowels /ɑː/, /ɔː/, /ɜː/, /ɪə/, /ɛə/, /ə/ occurs before another vowel, an /r/ is automatically inserted. Indeed this process is so automatic that speakers are usually unaware that they do it. Generally, too, we can say that the tendency is now so widespread that if speakers with a south-eastern-type English accent fail to use intrisuve /r/, especially after /ə/ or /ɪə/, they are very probably foreign. Many RP speakers, however, are careful not to use intrusive /r/ *within* words,

and will not say *drawing* /drɔːrɪŋ/, as many other non-RP speakers do
(but see p. 41).

Accents such as Scottish accents which have preserved post-vocalic
/r/ do not, of course, have intrusive /r/ (the analogical process does
not apply), and Scottish speakers often observe that 'English speakers
say *India* /ɪndɪər/'. English speakers, in fact, do not say /ɪndɪər/ but
they *do* say /ɪndɪər ən pɑːkɪstan/ *India and Pakistan*.

Loss of post-vocalic /r/ in RP and many other accents also means
that many words, such as *butter, better, hammer*, end in -/ə/ (rather
than -/ər/). When many new words such as *America, china, banana,
algebra* were adopted into the English language, there was in these
accents therefore no problem. They fitted into the same pattern and
were pronounced with final /ə/ – (with intrusive /r/, of course, if the
next word began with a vowel). However, in accents where post-
vocalic /r/ was preserved, there were no words ending in -/ə/, and
the problem therefore arose of how to incorporate these new words
into the English sound structure of these particular varieties. In many
Scottish accents the solution seems to have been to end words such as
these with /æ/ (the same vowel as in *hat*): /čʹainæ/ *china*. In accents in
the west of England, on the other hand, another solution was sometimes adopted and the new words assimilated to the pattern of
butter. We therefore find, in towns such as Southampton, pronunciations such as /bənʹænər/ *banana*, /vənʹɪlər/ *vanilla* and so on. (This is
not the same phenomenon as intrusive r, because in these accents the
r occurs even where there is a following consonant.) And in Bristol
the solution was to assimilate them to the pattern of *bottle, apple*
/ʹæpəl/. This is the so-called 'Bristol l' (see p. 78), as in *America*
/əmʹɛrɪkəl/, *Eva* /ʹiːvəl/, and so on.

Note that the actual pronunciation of /r/ also varies quite widely.
In Scotland, Wales and northern England a frequent pronunciation is
the flap [ɾ]; in the south-west of England and in Ireland a retroflex
approximant [ɻ] is used; and in south-eastern England the usual form
is the alveolar approximant [ɹ] also usual in RP. Other variants
include uvular [ʀ] in north-east England, and labio-dental [ʋ] from
younger speakers in the south. See also Chapter 5.

5 /uː/ and /ɔː/

We have already noted that Scottish and Northern Irish accents have
no distinction between /æ/ and /ɑː/. The same is also true, for the
most part, of the similar pairs of vowels /ʊ/ and /uː/, and /ɒ/ and /ɔː/.

Thus Scottish speakers make no distinction between pairs of words such as the following:

Pam	:	*palm*
pull	:	*pool*
cot	:	*caught*

6 /h/

Unlike RP, most urban regional accents in England and Wales do not have /h/, or are at least variable in its usage. For these speakers, therefore, *art* and *heart*, *arm* and *harm*, are pronounced the same. Speakers in the north-east of England, including Newcastle, do however retain /h/, as do Scottish and Irish speakers.

7 [ʔ]

RP speakers may use the glottal stop (see p. 39) word-initially before vowels: *ant* [ʔænt]: or before certain consonants or consonant clusters: *batch* [bæʔč], *six* [sɪʔks], *simply* [sɪmʔplɪ] (Brown, 1977).

In most British regional accents, however, the glottal stop is more widely used, particularly as an allophone of word-medial and word-final /t/. It is most common in the speech of younger urban working-class speakers, and is found in most regions, with the particular exception of many parts of Wales. It occurs much more frequently in some phonological contexts than others:

most frequent	*that man*	– finally before a consonant
	button	– before a syllabic nasal
	that apple	– finally before a vowel
	bottle	– before a syllabic /l/
least frequent	*better*	– before a vowel

(In the *that man* context, the glottal stop can also be heard from many RP speakers, as we have already noted.)

In some areas, especially the north-east of England, East Anglia, and Northern Ireland, the glottal stop may also be pronounced simultaneously with the voiceless stops /p/, /t/, /k/ in certain positions, most strikingly when between vowels:

flipper	[flˈɪp̰ə]
city	[sˈɪt̰iː]
flicker	[flˈɪk̰ə]

8 /ŋ/

(a) Most non-RP speakers of English, particularly in informal styles, do not have /ŋ/ in the suffix *-ing*. In forms of this type they have /n/ instead:

singing	/sˈɪŋɪn/
walking	/wˈɔːkɪn/

This pronunciation is also stereotypically associated (see also p. 40) with older members of the aristocracy, who are often caricatured as being particularly interested in huntin', shootin', and fishin'.

(b) In an area of western central England which includes Birmingham, Manchester and Liverpool, words which elsewhere have /ŋ/ and are spelt *ng* are pronounced with [ŋg]:

singer	[sɪŋgə]
thing	[θɪŋg]

9 /j/-dropping

At an earlier stage in the history of the English language, words like *rude* and *rule*, it is thought, were pronounced /rjuːd/, /rjuːl/. In modern English, however, the /j/, where it occurred after /r/, has been lost, and the pronunciation is now /ruːd/, /ruːl/. The same thing is true of earlier /juː/ after /l/: words such as *Luke*, which formerly had /j/, are today pronounced /luːk/ (except that some – particularly Scottish – accents still preserve /j/ in words like *illumine*, *allude*). Currently, too, /j/ is being lost after /s/: most speakers have *super* /sˈuːpə/, but many still retain /j/ in *suit* /sjuːt/, for example (see p. 42). In RP and many other English accents, though, this is as far as the process has gone, and /j/ can still occur before /uː/ after all other consonants. In certain regional accents, however, the change has progressed a good deal further. In parts of the north of England, for example, /j/ has been lost after /θ/, so that *enthuse* may be /ɛnθuːz/. In London, /j/ is very often lost after /n/: *news* may be /nuːz/ rather than RP-type /njuːz/. (And, as in a number of North American accents, /j/ can also, at least in northern areas of London, be lost after /t/ and /d/: *tune* /tuːn/, *duke* /duːk/, rather than /tjuːn/, /djuːk/ as in RP.) In a large area of eastern England, however, /j/ has been lost before /uː/ after *all* consonants. This area covers Norfolk and parts of Suffolk, Essex, Cambridgeshire, Northamptonshire, Bedfordshire, Leicestershire, Lincolnshire and Nottinghamshire, and includes the towns of Norwich, Ipswich, Cambridge and Peterborough. In this area pronunciations such as *pew* /pu:/, *beauty* /b'u:ti:/, *view* /vu:/, *few* /fu:/, *queue* /ku:/, *music* /m'u:zɪk/, *human* /h'u:mən/, are quite usual.

10 Long Mid Diphthonging

Accents in the south-eastern and southern-central part of England have undergone a process known as Long Mid Diphthonging (see Wells, 1982). This means that the vowels of *gate* and *boat* have a diphthongal character. Diphthongs may range from [æi] in *gate* and [æu] in *boat* in London and the south, through [ɛi] and [ɔu], to [ei] and [ou] (as in RP) in the north of the affected area. (That is, the more southerly the accent, the wider the diphthong.) In local accents elsewhere in the British Isles – the far south-west of England; the far north of England; Wales; Scotland; and Ireland – these vowels have retained older, non-diphthongal pronunciations such as [ge:t] and [bo:t].

Regional accent classification

To summarize the contents of this chapter, we can point out that the way in which most of the features we have been discussing are regionally distributed makes it possible to construct a classification of the major accent types to be found within the British Isles. This is illustrated in figure 4.3, which shows English accents divided into their main divisions and subdivisions, although note must be taken of the fact that the drawing of regional linguistic boundaries is a notoriously difficult and somewhat arbitrary task, and cases could certainly be made for different classifications than the ones we have used here. Note also that the political frontiers between Northern Ireland and the Republic of Ireland, between Scotland and England, and between England and Wales, do not coincide exactly with accent classification boundaries.

Figure 4.3 shows a division of English accents into five major groups in the British Isles: the south of England; the north of England; Wales; the south of Ireland; and Scotland and the north of Ireland. To help clarify the geographical positions of the subdivisions of the north of England and south of England groups, note the position of urban areas as follows:

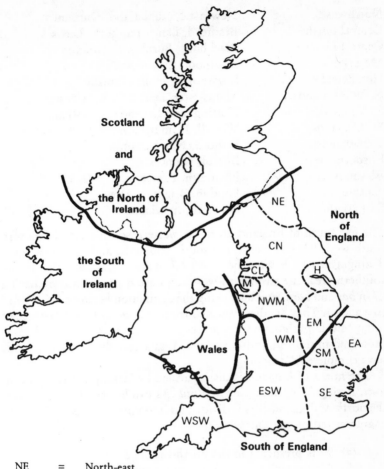

NE	=	North-east
CN	=	Central north
CL	=	Central Lancashire
M	=	Merseyside
H	=	Humberside
NWM	=	North-west Midlands
EM	=	East Midlands
WM	=	West Midlands
SM	=	South Midlands
ESW	=	Eastern south-west
WSW	=	Western south-west
SE	=	South-east
EA	=	East Anglia

Figure 4.3

North-east:	Newcastle, Sunderland, Durham
Central north:	Bradford, Lancaster, York, Leeds
Central Lancs.:	Blackburn, Burnley, Accrington
Merseyside:	Liverpool, Birkenhead
Humberside:	Scunthorpe, Hull, Grimsby
N. W. Midlands:	Manchester, Derby, Stoke, Chester
E. Midlands:	Nottingham, Leicester, Grantham
W. Midlands:	Walsall, Birmingham, Wolverhampton
S. Midlands:	Bedford, Northampton
E. south-west:	Bristol, Gloucester
W. south-west:	Plymouth, Exeter
South-east:	London, Brighton, Dover
East Anglia:	Norwich, Ipswich.

The five south of England areas the western south-west, the eastern south-west, the south-east, the south Midlands, and East Anglia are distinguished by having the vowel /ʌ/ in *putt*, and *cud*. Within the southern area, the two south-west areas are distinguished by having /r/ in *bar* and *bark*, and by lacking the distinction between /æ/ and /ɑː/ (see above). They are distinguished from each other by the absence of Long Mid Diphthonging in the western south-west. East Anglia has preserved initial /h/; and both East Anglia and the south Midlands have complete /j/-dropping.

The north of England is distinguished by lacking the vowel /ʌ/ in *putt*, having /ʊ/ in both *putt* and *put*. As can be seen from the map, the north of England area is divided up into nine sub-areas. These are characterized by the following features:

(a) /h/ is preserved in the north-east
(b) Words such as *singer* are pronounced with /ŋg/ in central Lancashire, Merseyside, the north-west Midlands, and the West Midlands
(c) Non-prevocalic /r/ is preserved in central Lancashire
(d) Words like *money* have final /iː/ in the north-east, Humberside, Merseyside, and west Midlands areas
(e) Long Mid Diphthonging in *gate* and *coat* occurs in Merseyside, the north-west Midlands, the east Midlands and the west Midlands (just as it does in the south of England)
(f) /j/-dropping is found in the east Midlands.

Ireland and Scotland lack Long Mid Diphthonging; they preserve /h/ and non-prevocalic /r/; and, like the south of England, they have /ʌ/ in *putt*. The north of Ireland and Scotland also lack the distinctions between /ʊ/ and /u:/, /æ/ and /ɑ:/, and /ɒ/ and /ɔ:/.

Wales is distinguished by lacking Long Mid Diphthonging, /h/ and non-prevocalic /r/; and by having /i:/ in *money*, /ʌ/ in *putt*, and /æ/ in *path* (though see Chapter 5).

For the summary of these facts, see table 4.2.

Table 4.2

	/ʌ/ in mud	/ɑ:/ in path	/ɑ:/ in palm	/i:/ in hazy	/r/ in bar	/u:/ in pool	/h/ in harm	/g/ in sing	/j/ in few	[ei] in gate
Scotland & N. Ireland	+	−	−	−	+	−	+	−	+	−
S. Ireland	+	+	+	+	+	+	+	−	+	−
North-east	−	−	+	+	−	+	+	−	+	−
Central N.	−	−	+	−	−	+	−	−	+	−
C. Lancs.	−	−	+	−	+	+	−	+	+	−
Merseyside	−	−	+	+	−	+	−	+	+	+
Humberside	−	−	+	+	−	+	−	−	+	−
N.W. Midlands	−	−	+	−	−	+	−	+	+	+
E. Midlands	−	−	+	−	−	+	−	−	−	+
W. Midlands	−	−	+	+	−	+	−	+	+	+
Wales	+	−	+	+	−	+	−	−	+	−
S. Midlands	+	+	+	+	−	+	−	−	−	+
E. South-west	+	−	−	+	+	+	−	−	+	+
W. South-west	+	−	−	+	+	+	−	−	+	−
South-east	+	+	+	+	−	+	−	−	+	+
East Anglia	+	+	+	+	−	+	+	−	−	+

5

British Isles accents and dialects

In this chapter we are going to look in greater detail at the speech of thirteen different areas of the British Isles. These correspond to the thirteen recordings of conversations on the tape which is available with the book. The speakers on the tape have quite distinct accents, and have been chosen to provide a sample of regional variation which is linguistically and geographically representative. The towns from which the first ten speakers come are: London (the speech and the speakers being known as 'cockney'); Norwich (East Anglia); Bristol (the west of England); Pontypridd (south Wales); Walsall (West Midlands); Bradford (Yorkshire); Liverpool (Merseyside); Edinburgh (Scotland); Belfast (Northern Ireland) and Dublin. We also investigate the English of three speakers of Traditional Dialect (see page 30) from the mainly rural county of Devon (south-west England), from Northumberland, and from the Lowlands of Scotland. The locations of these areas are shown on the map on page viii.

We shall treat each area in turn, indicating first the principal distinguishing features of the particular accent, and making reference where possible to examples of them in the recording (identified by line number in the transcript, e.g. l.10). Then follows an orthographic transcription of the relevant recording, and notes on interesting grammatical and lexical features which appear in the recording.

We should point out here, perhaps, that the recordings were not made by actors or in a studio. For the most part they are of people talking with friends in their own homes. In order to obtain speech which was natural, we wanted them to feel comfortable and relaxed, to speak as they usually would in friendly conversation. We think that in general we have achieved this. The conditions in which the recordings were made does mean, however, that there are occasions when people get excited, are interrupted, turn away from the micro-phone, or rattle a teacup in its saucer, and for this reason it is not always possible to decide just what is being said.

The recording for each of the first ten areas begins with the reading of a word list which is designed to bring out the principal differences between British Isles accents. For comparison, the very first recording on the tape is of an RP speaker reading that list. The list, together with the RP pronunciation of it, is given in the table on page xi (and is referred to subsequently as WL, with the number identifying the word, e.g. WL 5).

In the sections that follow we shall repeatedly want to speak about the qualities of different vowels. For example, in cockney, although the vowel /ʌ/, as in *cup*, is to be found in the same set of words as it is in RP, its realization (i.e. the actual sound made) is consistently different. To show these differences (which, of course, can be heard on the tape) we shall make use of vowel charts of the kind introduced in Chapter 3.

Figure 5.1

I. London

1   Cockney is, of course, a southern accent.

(a) /ʊ/ and /ʌ/ are both present and distinguish between, for
example, *put* and *putt* (WL 4, 5; see page 54–55). /ʌ/ is
realized as [æ̠] (figure 5.2, a clear example being *blood*, l. 11).

(b) /æ/ and /ɑː/ are distributed as in RP (WL 21–6; see p. 56). /æ/ is
realized as [ɛ̧], or as a dipthong, [ɛi] (figure 5.2; WL 21; *bag*, l.
37).

(c) Unlike RP, the final vowel of *city* etc. is /i/ and not /ɪ/ (WL 19,
20).

2   /h/ is almost invariably absent. When it is present, it is likely to be
in a stressed position (*happened*, l. 27).

3   The glottal stop, [ʔ], is extremely common in cockney speech. As
well as in the environments in which it occurs in RP, it is also
found:

(a) accompanying /p/ between vowels (*paper*, l. 2)

(b) representing /t/ between vowels and before pause (WL 1–6
etc.; *butterfly*, l. 20; *wet*, l. 3).

4   (a) The contrast between /θ/ and /f/ is variably lost;

initially	*thin*	/fɪn/
medially	*Cathy*	/kæfiː/
finally	*both*	/bouf/

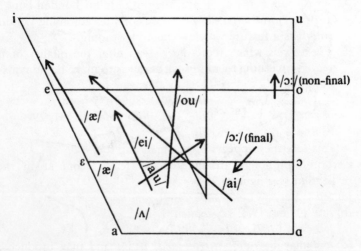

Figure 5.2 Typical realizations of certain cockney vowels

(b) Similarly, the contrast between /ð/ and /v/ is also often lost:
    medially   *together*   /təgɛvə/, (l. 21)
    and finally   *bathe*   /beiv/
Initially, /d/ or zero is more likely to be heard for /ð/
e.g. *the* (l. 4) is /də/
     they (l. 11) is /ei/

5 (a) When /ɔː/ is final it is realized much as the vowel of *pore* in
       some RP speech; when /ɔː/ is non-final, its realization is much
       closer, [oː] (figure 5.2; cf. WL 45, 48).
   (b) As a result of this difference, there is a distinction made in the
       speech of London and of areas to the south of the city, which
       is absent in RP, between pairs of words like:
       paws [pɔəz] and *pause* [poːz] (WL 48, 49)
       bored [bɔəd] and *board* [boːd]
   The distinction is made on the basis of the presence or absence of
   inflection. Where, for example, plural, third person singular, or
   genitive *s* is added to a word-final /ɔː/, [ɔə] is still found, rather
   than [ɔː].

6 (a) When /l/ occurs finally after a vowel e.g. *Paul* (WL 30), *well*
       (l. 19); before a consonant in the same syllable e.g. *milk*; or as
       a syllable in itself e.g. *table*, it is realized as a vowel. Thus:
       [pou, wɛʊ, mɪʊk, tæɪbʊ]. When the preceding vowel is /ɔː/,
       there may be complete loss of /l/. Thus *Pauls* may be [poːz],
       i.e. identical with *pause*.
       These comments on /l/ are true not only for London but also
       for the Home Counties i.e. those counties adjoining London,
       and it is a feature which seems to spreading.
   (b) The vowels which represent /l/ can alter the quality of the
       vowels preceding them in such a way as to make homonyms of
       pairs like:
       pool   *pull*   (WL 28, 29)
       doll   *dole*   (cf. *doll*, *pole*, WL 31, 29)
       peal   *pill*
   This tendency appears to be spreading too.

7 Certain diphthongs are markedly different from RP in their
   realization (see figure 5.2).
   (a) /ei/ is [æɪ] (WL 40; *paper*, l. 2)
   (b) /ou/ is [æʉ] (WL 12; *soaked*, l. 10)
   (c) /ai/ is [ɑɪ] (WL 9; *inside*, l. 3)
   (d) /au/ may be [æə] (*surrounded*, l. 54) and may produce an
       intrusive /r/ (see p. 60) as *now*, l. 57.

8   -*ing* is /ɪn/
    (a) *laying*, (l. 1) (see p. 63)
    (b) In *nothing*, *something* etc. -*ing* may be [ɪŋk] (*anything*, l. 5)
9   When they are initial, /p, t, k/ are heavily aspirated, more so than
    in RP. In the case of /t/, there is affrication (the tongue leaves the
    alveolar ridge slowly and [s] is produced before the vowel begins).
    Thus *tea*, l. 5, is [tsiː].

The recording

The speaker is a working man of about fifty who has lived all his life
in London. His accent is quite strong, though certain features, such
as the use of /f/ for /θ/, are not so obvious. He is talking about his
time in hospital just before his release after an operation.

The reader of the word list is younger and her accent is not as
strong. Notice the variability in the realization of final /t/, which is
sometimes [ʔ] and sometimes [t].

I came back to the bed, like, after breakfast . . . I was just like laying
on it a bit and reading th . . . the paper, and, I don't know, I thought
to myself, I don't know, I feel wet in my pyjamas and I looked inside
. . . and put my hand in it . . . it is wet wh . . . how . . . how the
5   dickens . . . I ain't spilt any tea or anything down there. So I thought
to myself, I know, I'll go out in the ablution place, like, there . . .
they've got some little radiators . . . all little individual places . . .
got a little radiator there . . . put my pyjamas on to dry, I just
thought it was some water . . . of course when I go out there the
10 dressing that was on me, that was soaked in a . . . yeh, like a . . . a
watery blood . . . so, course I went and saw the sister and er . . . they
put another dressing on it . . . they put another dressing on it . . . yeh
. . . yeh . . . it wasn't . . . wasn't long before that was soaked and all,
Fred . . . wasn't long before that was soaked . . . so of course I went
15 and had another one done . . . so I said to the . . . the nurse, I said –
guess to what it was – it was like where they . . . they'd taken the
tubes out, and I said to her have they opened up? She said no, there's
nothing, like o . . . a . . . actually open . . . it's seeping . . . it was
seeping through it, yeh. Well . . . I said, well I said, if you put s . . .
20 some, like, little butterfly stitches over that first of all . . . out of . . .
er . . . er . . . plaster like . . . you know . . . hold that together. I said
well then . . . put a dressing and a big plaster on it, so she done that,

but it still didn't . . . yeh . . . it still seeped through . . . and course I
begin to get worried, and when . . . when she done it, like, the third
time . . . took if off – I'm laying there – I could see it, it was running
away from me like tears. Yeh . . . but yeh, but anyway. . . yeh . . . yeh
. . . that's what I say. . . and of course, what . . . what had happened,
also, that was the Saturday, wasn't it?, yeh, I . . . er . . . had my
pyjamas . . . I . . . I'd just changed my pyjamas so I said to Rene, I
phoned Rene there, and I said, could you bring me another one of my
old pairs of pyjamas, I said, cos, I said, some stain had come through
it, you know, how, you know . . . round the waistband and that. So
she brought me in a new pair of 'jamas in the afternoon and I went
and changed them and . . . and that . . . but, blimey, before she went
home, they were worse than the other pair, weren't they? It'd come
through and it had soaked right through and down the leg, and the
other pair had dried off a bit in the bag so I thought, well, I'll have to
keep them, so . . . I did get it done again and er . . . I changed into
pyjamas . . . well of course when it come to the Sunday, I'm going
home Sunday, made arrangements for . . . she's going to pick me up
about ten . . . so of course I had to see the . . . the sister . . . and er
. . . she said I'd like the doctor to see that . . . well . . . time's going
on, so I phoned Rene in the morning and said don't pick me up at
ten, make it nearer twelve, sort of thing . . . it'd give me a chance . . .
and er . . . anyway. . . it was a long while before this doctor come up.
It was only, like, the young one, see, weekend one. But anyway, the
sister, she was getting a bit worried. She said he don't seem to be
coming, so she had a look, and she said, well if it was my decision she
wouldn't let me home . . . and er . . . anyhow I more or less pleaded
with her, I said well they're coming here in a little while, I said, if
you'd've told me before, I said, I would have made arrangements and
cancelled it . . . anyway. . . she was still worried so she went and she
found this young doctor. He come along . . . still laying there, you
know, on my bed, sort of thing, surrounded. Eventually he comes ten
to twelve . . . and he has a look and . . . he's, like, with the nurse
there, he wasn't with the sister, but anyway he said, well, he said, you
don't seem to be weeping now . . . he said, I don't think it'll weep any
more, he said . . . erm . . . he said, well, if I let you go home, he said,
he said, they'll have to be dressed twice a day . . . he said, and he said
. . . twice a day, he said, while it's . . . comes away a bit wet, he said,
and once a day, he said, when it's dry, sort of thing.

Notes

1 The past tense of COME is variably *came* e.g. l. 1 and *come* e.g. l. 39, 45, 53 (see p. 24).

2 The past tense of the full verb DO is *done* (l. 20, 24; see p. 24).

3 First person singular, negative, of the auxiliary *have* is *ain't* (l. 5; see p. 23).

4 Third person singular, negative, of the auxillary *do* is *don't* (l. 47; see p. 26).

5 The use of *lay* for standard English *lie* (l. 1) is not restricted to any region, and Standard English speakers often seem to have to concentrate hard to produce the appropriate form!

6 Items like *and all* (meaning, *as well*) (l. 13), *like* (throughout), *and that* (l. 34), are also not restricted to any particular region, and are best regarded simply as features of colloquial speech.

7 Exclamations like *how the dickens* (l. 4) and *blimey* (l. 34) are colloquial, found in a number of regions of Britain, and probably used more by older people.

8 *cos* (l. 32) represents /kɒz/, a colloquial form of *because*.

II. Norwich

1 The speech of Norwich in particular, and East Anglia in general, is southern.

(a) /ʊ/ and /ʌ/ are both present (WL 4, 5)

(b) /æ/ and /ɑ:/ are distributed as in RP (WL 21–6)

(c) the final vowel of *city* etc. is /i/, not /ɪ/ as in RP (WL 19, 20). But it differs from the accents of London and the Home Counties (see p. 71) in that /l/ in *milk*, *pull*, *bottle* etc. is not realized as a vowel. Rather, like RP, there is a 'dark' /l/, [ɫ], with the back of the tongue raised towards the soft palate (WL 27–31).

2 In Norfolk and neighbouring areas (see p. 63) /j/ is variably lost after all consonants (*humorous*, l. 1).

3 An older English distinction, lost in RP, is maintained. Thus RP homonyms are quite distinct in Norwich.

/u:/	/ɔu/
moan	*mown*
sole	*soul*
nose	*knows* (WL 38, 39)

4 For some speakers, words like *moon* and *boot* have the same vowel (/u:/) as *moan* and *boat*, such pairs being homonyms (WL 11, 12).

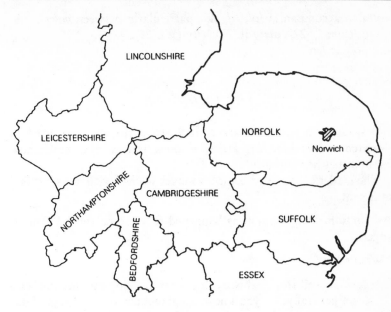

Figure 5.3

5 The RP distinction between /ɪə/ and /ɛə/ is not present, and so, for example, both *beer* and *bear* are pronounced /bɛ:/ (WL 14, 15; *hear*, l. 23; *here*, l. 20).

6 While /h/ has been preserved in rural East Anglia, it has been partly lost in Norwich. Thus in the recording it is generally present in stressed words e.g. *humorous* (l. 1) and *husband* (l. 25), but sometimes missing in unstressed words. Note (l. 30) that, within a second, *he* is produced first with /h/ and then without.

7 Certain words which have /ou/ in RP may have /ʊ/, e.g. *home* (l. 31) and *suppose* (l. 45).

8 Words like *room* and *broom*, and (as in other eastern accents – see p. 55) *roof* and *hoof*, have /ʊ/ rather than /u:/.

9 Stressed vowels are long, while unstressed vowels are much reduced, giving a distinctive rhythm to East Anglian speech. Associated with the reduction of unstressed vowels is the loss of consonants e.g. the loss of /v/ in *side of it* (l. 19).

10 *off* is /ɔ:f/ (l. 27).

11 The glottal stop [ʔ] variably represents /t/ between vowels, and

also accompanies /p/, /t/, /k/, particularly between vowels e.g. *bottom* (l. 22), *dirty* (l. 27), *city* (WL 19).

12   *–ing* is /ən/.

The recording

The speaker is a woman about fifty years old who has lived in Norwich all her life. Her accent is quite strong. She recalls how she first met her husband.

The reader of the word list is a younger woman with not so strong an accent.

I've got something humorous happened to me, one thing I'll never forget.

– What's that?

Eh? We . . . well th . . . this is, this is when I first met my husband
5   . . . cos I generally . . . you know, my daughter always laugh about that, we went and had a drink . . . erm . . . one night. I don't know if you know the Blue Room? near the erm . . . do you know the . . . erm . . . Yeh.

Well we went in there one night to have a drink. There was erm . . .
10   two girl friends and me . . . this was before I married, see and, well this was the night, see, when I met my husband and erm you know they was like b . . . the fellows was buying us drinks and that, see, and er my friend and her sister, oh, she say, we don't want to go with them, she said, let's give them the slip . . . right . . . well we ran up er
15   Prince of Wales Road and opposite the, well, that's . . . that was the Regent then, that's the ABC now, there's a fruiterers, Empire Fruit Stores, I don't know if it's still there, is it? Well there was this here fruits . . . er . . . fruitstore and that and they had a passage way at the side of it, see. Well my friends said to me, oh, they said, Flo we'll get
20   in here and give them the slip . . . I went to go in first . . . thought that was a long passage and that wasn't . . . they had forty steps and I fell right to the bottom . . . yeh . . . and there was me, see, and we . . . and we could hear . . . y'know they could hear these here fellows come run . . . running up behind, see, so my friends said, oh quick,
25   Flo have fell down a lot of stairs. Well the one what's my husband, he said, let her lay there, he said. We've been treating you all night, they said, and you do us the dirty and run off . . . and they let me lay

there. Well, any rate my friends, I managed to stumble up. I had two
big bumps on my head . . . I had a black eye . . . and course erm the
30 . . . erm . . . see . . . my husband to be then erm he well he let me lay
there well when I got home, see, my father said to me, the first thing
. . . whatever have you done? I said, I got knocked down by a bike . . .
that was the first thing that come into my head . . . yeh and I . . . I
gen . . . generally tell my daughter about that. I said . . . she say,
35 that's what you get, Mum, she say, for making a fellow, she said
letting a fellow, she said, buy you the drink and then, she said,
running away from him. I say yeh, but that, you know, that's sort
of like . . . well then he come round the next night to see how I was
and that's how we got acquainted. He said, that'll teach you . . . he
40 said, er yeh, he said, that'll teach you, he say . . . taking drinks off
anyone he said and try, he said, you thought, he said, you were going
to slip off, he said . . . erm . . . he said, did you know there was any
steps? and I said, no I didn't . . . I thought that was a long passage,
see, and there was just, there was forty steps that go right down I
45 suppose to . . . and lead into a door at the back of this here fruit
shop.

Notes

1 The third person singular, present tense is not marked by /s/. Thus: *laugh*
   (l. 5), *say* (l. 13, 34, 40; see p. 26).
2 The absence of /s/ applies also to auxiliary *have* (l. 25).
3 Introduction of a relative clause by *what* (l. 25; see p. 27).
4 *lay* (l. 26): Standard English *lie* (as in the London recording).
5 *that* is used where standard English would have *it* (l. 37).
6 Note intrusive /r/ in *by a bike* [bəɹəbaɪk̚?] (l. 32; see p. 60).

III. Bristol

1 The speech of Bristol, and the south-west generally, makes a
   distinction between pairs like *put* and *putt* (WL 4, 5). The vowel
   of *putt*, however, is [ə], and it seems that, unlike in RP, there are
   not two distinct phonemes /ə/ and /ʌ/ (see p. 55).
2 There is no /æ/–/ɑː/ contrast (WL 21–26), and /æ/ is realized as [a]
   (figure 5.5 and figure 4.1)
3 (a) There is post-vocalic /r/ (see p. 58 and figure 4.2). /r/ is quite
       retroflex in quality (see p. 61), that is, with the tip of the

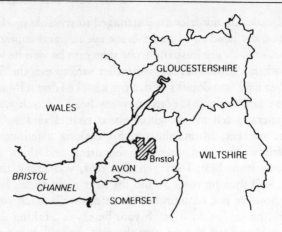

Figure 5.4

tongue bending backwards towards the hard palate (WL 14–18, 34–7, 42–4; note contrast with 45). Note that the equivalents to the RP diphthongs /ɪə/, /ɛə/, and /ʊə/ are /ɪr/ (WL 14), /ɛr/ (WL 15), and /ur/ (WL 42).

(b) A feature of speech known as 'Bristol l', which is confined to the immediate area of Bristol, is the presence of /l/ following word final /ə/. Thus *America* may be /əmɛrɪkəl/ and *Eva* /iːvəl/. In such cases *Eva* and *evil* are homophones. Bristol l is not so common, generally stigmatized, and cannot be heard on our recording (see p. 61).

(c) Notice that dark /l/ (see p. 41) is very dark, that is, the raising of the back of the tongue to soft palate is most marked.

4　There is a tendency, though probably less common than in London, for the contrast between /θ/ and /f/ to be lost, but again there is no example of this on our recording.

5　The glottal stop [ʔ] may represent [t] before pause e.g. *Pete*, [piːʔ] (l. 18) (but note that in l. 13), *Pete* is [piːt]).

6　The diphthongs /ei/ and /ou/ are rather wide, [ɛi] and [ɔu] (figure 5.5 and WL 8, 40, 41, and 29, 38, 39).

7　*–ing* is /ɪn/.

8　As in London speech, in words like *anything*, *something*, *–ing* may be /ɪŋk/ (l. 3, *something*).

9　(a) By comparison with RP, short vowels are often of longer duration. Thus: *job* [jɑ·b] (l. 38), *mad* [ma·d] (l. 12), and *bucket* [bə·kɪ·ʔ] (l. 61).

(b) In certain words there is a stronger vowel than its equivalent in RP, e.g. /gʊdnɛs/ (l. 36) as opposed to /gʊdnəs/, or /gʊdnɪs/ in RP.

(c) Similarly, a vowel followed by a consonant is found where in RP there is a syllabic consonant, e.g. ['bə?ən] as opposed to [bʌtn̩] *button*.

10 /h/ is variably absent. Thus, (l. 3), it is present four times in succession (*He'd had his fixed, he said*), but is absent on the next occasion (l. 4), where *had* is [ad].

The recording

The speaker is a housewife, about thirty years old. Though she quite clearly comes from the Bristol area, her accent is less broad than most on the tape. As mentioned above, local features of pronunciation seem to become more frequent when she becomes excited.

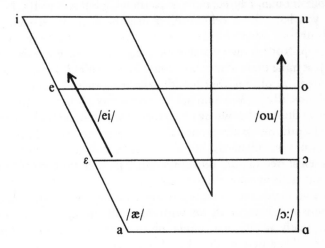

Figure 5.5 Typical realizations of certain vowels in Bristol speech

You know . . . our overflow . . . well it does overf . . . well a fortnight ago, next door neighbour said to us – mind, his overflows every day – erm . . . could Pete do something about it. He'd had his fixed, he said. So Pete came in and went up and had a look it's it's the . . . erm 5 . . . you know, the immersion heater system. I think it's where the ball thing doesn't close up properly, so the water drips out the

overflow. Well that was fair enough. Pete came up and had a go at it
and ever since then two days apart from yesterday it's the only time
ours has dripped out at all. Every day of the week theirs's dripped
10 out. So yesterday afternoon Pete comes home from fishing. I'm sure
he waited for Pete, because he knows Pete won't say anything, see,
cos I was mad . . . and er Pete comes in, and I heard all these doors
going and I went out and the hot water tap was on so I said: Who's
turned the hot water tap on? Pete said: He's just asked me again, can
15 I do something about our overflow because it was pouring out
yesterday; something had gone really wrong yesterday, the thing
wasn't working at all. So I said: Well you did tell him that his
hasn't stopped since he said. No, says Pete. He's moaning about
ours overflowing. Mine overflows into the bunker, mind, my bun-
20 ker, and flows out. And this morning I come down, and blow me if
this isn't isn't overflowing again, this one. I was mad. When Pete
went I couldn't even watch the film I was watching. I was so mad. I
thought, well the least Pete could have done was said: Well, look, you
know fair enough, I agree, mine is overflowing but so's yours. I mean,
25 would you have the cheek to tell a neighbour to mend something
when your own wasn't fixed . . . well it's our water that's making his
wall damp. Not his own water, mind, that flows out every day of the
week. Just mine that's done three times in a fortnight. I was mad, Jill,
really mad . . . oh, no, that was the guttering that . . . and that was
30 his fault as well . . . no no no ne . . . no cos tha . . . it runs from ours
down next door and down again to their drain. No, it was his cos he's
never cleaned his gutters out. Us, thinking we were being good
cleaned ours out regularly, but all we really did, see, it built up, the
water then stayed in ours because it didn't go over the top of the dirt.
35 Yeh. That is fixed now, though, since Pete got up there, that's been
perfectly all right, even with the heavy weather, thank goodness. Do
have these problems, don't we, with these silly things . . . I mean the
point is, really, it's quite a simple job to fix it. Pete's Dad said really
all you need is a new washer, but, I don't know where your . . . erm
40 . . . immersion, you know, your tank is but ours is high in the airing
cupboard. The shelf that's in the airing cupboard won't support the
weight of anybody, and from outside you can't get your head up and
over the top. Well . . . no no, and it means that Pete's got to s . . .
kind of get up and over, well, what's worrying me is, you've got to
45 turn the water off, well that's fair enough but my fire heats the water,
well if he can just take the arm off, replace the washer and put it
back, that's good, but if anything goes wrong I've then got to let the

fire out, because I can't have the fire going if the water can't be
replaced and so what is really a simple job, knowing us, could take
50 all day. So I'd rather it dripped out there a bit longer . . . nothing. He
reckoned he had somebody in, but, I mean, if I had somebody in I
would expect the job done properly, I mean, fair enough, Pete's just
bent our arm, well, his dad said that won't last long because, you
know, a couple of weeks and the arm'll naturally put itself back up.
55 He said it's the new washer, but course it was doing a new washer
down at the church that Pete's dad chopped all his hand the other
week and had to have a week off work. And it's thinking of things
like that that can happen to people who don't usually have calamities
that makes me a bit worried about letting Pete do ours . . . oh well I
60 . . . I expect so. It was this morning I went out this morning to fill my
coal bucket, it wa . . . well I don't I don't feel I should complain,
because mine does drip out now and then, but knowing his does it
every day . . . I mean it's a bit off in't it Jill . . . anyway . . . but I will
get ours fixed in due course . . . but when I'm sure it isn't going to
65 cause a calamity at the same time.

Notes

1 Notice the infrequency of fillers like *kind of*, and *like*.
2 *drips out the overflow* (l. 6) cf. Standard English, *out of the overflow*
  (see p. 30).
3 *course* (l. 55) = *of course*.

IV. South Wales (Pontypridd)

1 In South Wales the distribution of /æ/ and /ɑ:/ is generally as in
  the north of England (see p. 53 and figure 4.1). The contrast
  between the vowels, however, is usually one of length only. Thus
  cat [kat] and *cart* [ka:t] (WL 21, 26).
2 (a) There is no post-vocalic /r/, except in the speech of some
      native speakers of Welsh (figure 4.2).
  (b) /r/ is normally a flap [ɾ] (see p. 61), that is, the tip of the
      tongue makes a rapid tap against the alveolar ridge (as in the
      speech of some RP speakers in the pronunciation of words like
      very and *marry* (e.g. *tramline*, *right*, l. 2).
3 As in Bristol, there is not a /ʌ/–/ə/ contrast. Words like *putt* (WL
  5) have /ə/, contrasting with /ʊ/ in *put* (WL 4).

English accents and dialects

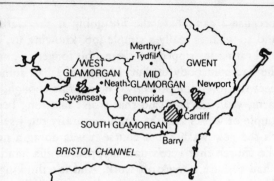

Figure 5.6

4   Words like *city* and *seedy* have /iː/ as the final vowel (WL 19, 20).

5   /l/ is not 'dark' in any environment (WL 27–31).

6   In words like *tune*, *few*, *used*, we find /ɪu/ rather than /juː/ (*used*, l. 1). This diphthong is preserved even after /r/ and /l/. Thus most speakers make a distinction between pairs such as *blew* /blɪu/ and *blue* /bluː/, *threw* and *through*. *Blew* and *blue* are contrasted in the short exchange at the end of the word list (see p. 63 and figure 5.7).

7   Between vowels, when the first vowel is stressed, consonants may be doubled. So *city* (WL 19) is [sˈɪtiː].

8   /h/ is usually absent, but may be present in stressed positions e.g. *him*, l. 25.

9   (a) /ei/ is narrow and may even be a monophthong [eˑ] (figure 5.7 WL 8, 40, 41).

    (b) In certain areas of Wales a distinction is made between pairs of words like *daze*/deiz/ and *days*/dɛɪz/. /ɛɪ/ occurs where there is *i* or *y* in the spelling. The speakers on the tape do not make this distinction.

10   /ou/ is narrow and may even be a monophthong [oː] (WL 12, 29, 38, 39). This tendency may result in such pairs as *so* and *soar* being homonyms.

11   The vowel /ɜː/, as in *bird* (WL 16), is produced with the lips rounded, approaching [øː].

12   Intonation in Welsh English is very much influenced by the Welsh language. Though quite noticeable in the recording, it is less striking than in the speech of many Welsh people, including those whose first language is English. Welsh is learned

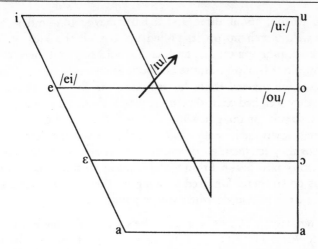

Figure 5.7 Typical realizations of certain South Wales vowels

as a first language normally only in the west and north-west of the country.

The recording

The speaker is a young man from Pontypridd, whose accent, though quite obviously Welsh, is not particularly strong. He is talking about an accident that happened to someone as a child.

The word list reader is a young woman from Neath. Again, although she is clearly Welsh, her accent is not very strong.

At the end of the word list there is the following exchange to demonstrate the difference between *blew* and *blue*:

What did the wind do yesterday?
Erm . . . the wind blew /blɪu/ strongly.
All right . . . and what colour are your jeans?
My jeans are blue /blu:/.

The tramlines . . . ah, they used to have . . . erm . . . from the pit there used to be a tramline right to the top of the mountain . . . used to work on a . . . a pulley sort of system, I should think, I was too young to know then. They used to have about fifteen to twenty big pit drams on this wire rope, and I would say it must have stretched,

5

bottom to top, about three and a half, maybe four miles, and of
course we'd winch up on it, pulled up, cos all the kids would be
running up, jumping on . . . and, er, I would say, well there was one
boy, how old is Gevin . . . must be about thirty-eight he's . . . jumped
10   on and he fell off and it cut his leg clean off. But they're big metal
drams, they weighed well, they must weigh about a ton with nothing
in them, so you can imagine when they're full . . . and of course when
they come down the journey again . . . they're coming down at a fair
speed cos they let them go down quite a bit and then they got them
15   . . . on automatic brake, I think, and it slows them down . . . we used
to come down there. We used to jump on them on the top and ride
down . . . things you do when you're young . . .

About ten, twelve . . . he won't . . . he's got a false leg but he won't
wear it. When he wears it, you know . . . when he first had it he
20   used to wear it . . . and er, he was quite a big boy, as all Welshmen
are, they're all broad, but he must be up to . . . something like . . .
twenty-eight stone and he's really fat, it just hangs off him. He sits
and watches television and he has two pound of apples and er say a
pound of chocolate . . . and . . . his mother makes sandwiches, she
25   makes a loaf of bread . . . just for him, for sandwiches, as a snack
. . . well most of the boys who drink with him in the club . . . erm
. . . were with Gevin when he done it . . . when he done it . . . they
used all used to ride up on the . . . the journey, aye I should think
every boy in Cil has done it.

30   – You did it, did you?

Oh, aye, regular.

We'd always be warned – don't ride on the drams . . . [Welsh] . . .
straight down the bottom and wait for them to come up and you'd
you'd run up along side them and just jump on . . . the most dangerous
35   thing about that was . . . er . . . was the rope, the metal rope, which was
about two inches in diameter, and it used to whip. And of course you
imagine a steel rope whipping . . . well it'd cut a man clean in half . . .
you never see the dangers when you're young, do you?

Notes

1   *Two pound of apples* (l. 23) see p. 30.
2   *Done* as past tense of DO (l. 27) see p. 25.
3   *Aye = yes* (l. 28): common in the north of England, Scotland, Ireland and
    Wales.

Figure 5.8

V. West Midlands

This is the accent spoken in Birmingham, Wolverhampton, and a number of other towns in that area (see map).

1　The accent of the West Midlands is northern in that:
 (a) /æ/ is found in words such as *dance, daft* etc. (see p. 56; WL 21–6)
 (b) Pairs of words like *put* and *putt* are not distinct, /ʊ/ being the vowel in both (see p. 54; WL 4, 5).

2　The accent nevertheless has certain southern characteristics:
 (a) The final vowel of *city* and *seedy* etc. is /iː/ (see p. 57; WL 19, 20; cf. Liverpool)
 (b) The diphthongs /ei/ and /ou/ are wide, being realized as [æɪ] and [ʌʊ] (figure 5.9; WL 8, 40, 41 and 12, 29, 38, 39).

3　/iː/ is [ɜi] (figure 5.9; WL 14, 19, 20).
 /uː/ is [ɛu] (figure 5.9; WL 28).

4　/ai/ is [ɔi] (figure 5.9; WL 9, 46, 47).

5　/ɪ/ is very close, (figure 5.9; WL 1, 19).

6　/ɜː/ and /ɛə/ are merged as [œː] e.g. *bear* and *bird* on the word list. The influence of RP is, however, discernible in the attempted distinction on the word list between *fur* and *fair*. This merger is not found throughout the West Midlands (figure 5.9).

7　/h/ is usually absent.

8　*–ing* is /ɪn/.

9　Note *one* is /wɒn/ but *won* is /wʊn/ (l. 25; see p. 55).

10　There are few glottal stops.

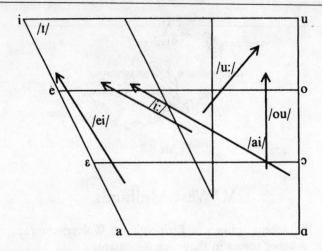

Figure 5.9 Typical realizations of certain West Midlands vowels

The recording

The speaker, who is a caretaker, is from Walsall and has a very distinctive West Midlands accent. After saying something about his evening habits, he goes on to talk about his footballing days and then about the problems of Walsall Football Club.

I don't go out much, not in the week, you know. I go out one night a week, and if the wife isn't bothered. I won't, you know, I don't bother. Well, the wife and the daughter generally go out together and I stop in, you know, with the lad . . . but er as g . . . the wife and
5 the daughter they've booked up a show what the women have got up or something, eight fifty to see that man who works . . . impersonates a woman . . . what's his name him who impersonates the women on the television . . .

The other night I couldn't get in . . . interested in it about ho . . .
10 homosexuals, you know, and I said to my wife, I says, er, are you coming to bed? Her says, no. I'm going to see the finish of this. I says, all right then, goodnight, and I went up to bed. I mean . . . I'm not, you know, like that . . .

I used to be keen. I used to be a good footballer myself . . . yeh . . .
15 Goodyears and all those, you know, they was high class teams, I

mean you played for the honour then, I mean, you didn't get nothing out of it . . .

No, no, well, er me and the captain of Guest Keens, we had a trial for Walsall and er we came up the one week and they says, come the next week and play again, see, well in the meantime we've got an important match for the works team, cup final, and the captain says, are you going to Walsall? I said no, the works team's more important to me, see. Course we didn't go, and we had a nasty post card off Walsall FC about it, cos we didn't turn up . . .

Well I won the one cup for them really in . . . erm . . . 1948 . . . er we was er winning one-none half time, and the second half I got three goals, and we won four . . . a . . . an theys . . . and they made me go and have the cup, cos, they said, you've won this cup and you're going to have it, and I . . . I . . . present . . . presented with it, you know. . .

I could have done, yes, If I'd have stuck to it, you know, but . . . er . . . well . . . when, you know . . . no, no . . . but I mean, you didn't get a lot then if you played professional, I mean, it was a poor wage then, years ago . . . but it . . . it was an honour to play, they didn't play for the money like they do today. . . well, they've got to make it while they're fit, cos you never know what's going to happen . . .

Well Dave Mackay was on the wireless this morning before I come out, you know, and they was interviewing him, the reporter, and he said he . . . he couldn't understand it why they couldn't score at home . . . I mean, but win away, you know. . . played for Derby, half-back, didn't he? Yes, I do. I always like to see them win, and that, but er . . . something . . . lacking there, definitely . . .

Well Walsall can if they dish the football up. Course they couldn't keep me away years ago. I used to go to every . . . well, I think it's been about six or eight years, when they played Sunderland down here in the cup, and Liverpool . . . I paid a man to do my job, here of a Saturday afternoon to go and see the two matches. And when I come back . . . I was away, say, two hours . . . I'd still got the same work to do . . . nothing had been done . . .

Well er they never spent no money but they got local talent . . . they got a lot of local talent what come up . . . you know, like . . . out of the amateur sides. That's where they go wrong, they don't go to the proper matches . . . er . . . like Shrewsbury, now, Chick Bates, they had him from Stourbridge for about two hundred and fifty pound fee

55 . . . and he's scoring two or three goals a match now . . . I mean,
Walsall could've done with a man like him.

Notes

1 There are examples of multiple negation (see p. 22):
    You didn't get nothing out of it (l. 16).
    Well they never spent no money (l. 49).
2 Past tense of COME is *come* (l. 37, 47, 50).
3 (a) *I says* (l. 10) is 'present historic' (see p. 27).
   (b) *was* is the past tense form of BE, not only for the third person
   singular:
       We was winning (l. 25)
       they was interviewing him (l. 37).
4 *What* introduces a relative clause (see p. 27):
    they got a lot of local talent what come up (l. 50).
5 *something* (l. 41) is /sʊmət/.
6 (a) *not bothered* (l. 2) = not keen.
   (b) *the lad* (l. 4) i.e. his son cf. *the wife*
   (c) *FC* (l. 24) = Football Club.
   (d) *wireless* (l. 36) is not regional but old-fashioned. It bears the same
   relationship to *radio* as *gramophone* does to *record player* (see p. 11).
7 *postcard off Walsall FC* (l. 20) = Standard English: *from Walsall FC* (see
   p. 30).
8 *you* is /jaʊ/.
9 Dave Mackay (l. 36) is a former Scottish international footballer, and
   manager of Walsall at time of recording.
10 *her* (l. 11) = *she*.
11 The definite article before a vowel is /ð/ e.g. *th' amateur* (l. 51).

VI. Bradford

1 The accent of Bradford, and of Yorkshire generally, is northern in
   that:
   (a) Words like *dance* and *daft* have /æ/ (WL 22, 23; see p. 56). For
       some Yorkshire speakers, /æ/ and /ɑ:/ are differentiated only
       by length. For them the vowels are [a] and [a:] (figure 5.11),
       Pam and *palm* being [pam] and [pa:m]. This is not the case for
       the speakers on the tape, for whom /ɑ:/ is a little further back
   (b) There is no distinction between pairs of words like *put* and
       putt, both having /ʊ/ (WL 4, 5; see p. 54)
   (c) The final vowel in words like *city* and *seedy* is /ɪ/ (WL 19, 20;
       see p. 57).

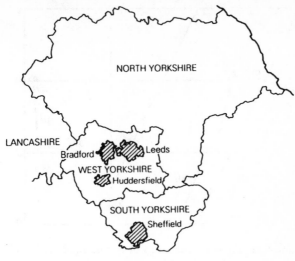

Figure 5.10

2 (a) (i) /ei/ is either a narrow diphthong or a monophthong, [e:] (e.g. *plate*, WL 40; *mate*, WL 52; figure 5.11).

      (ii) But for some speakers, words which have *eigh* in the spelling (e.g. *weight*, WL 41) have /eɪ/ (figure 5.11).

  (b) (i) /ou/ is also a narrow diphthong or a monophthong, [o̞:] (e.g. *boat*, WL 12; *nose*, WL 38; figure 5.11).

      (ii) But, for some speakers, many words which have *ow* or *ou* in the spelling (e.g. *knows*, WL 39) have /ɔu/ (figure 5.11). Thus for these speakers *nose* and *knows* are not homonyms. This distinction (also made in Norwich – see p. 74) is being lost, younger speakers generally using /ou/ for both sets of words.

3 Pairs of words like *pore* (which has *r* in the spelling) and *paw* (WL 44, 45) are distinguished. Words without *r* have /ɔ:/ ([ɔ̞:]); words with *r* have /ɔə/ ([ɔ̞ə]) (figure 5.11). This distinction is also made by some RP speakers.

4 (a) /ɛ/ is [ɛ̞] i.e. more open than in southern accents (WL 2; figure 5.11).

  (b) /u:/ is [u:] as compared with the more central realization of this vowel in Lancashire (WL 28; figure 5.11).

  (c) /ai/ is [aɛ] (WL 46; figure 5.11).

5 In West Yorkshire (which includes Bradford) and other areas of

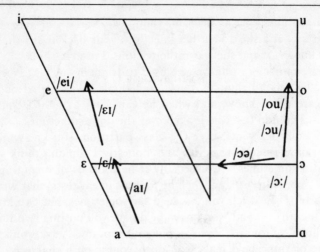

Figure 5.11 Typical realizations of certain Bradford vowels

Yorkshire, /b, d, g/ become /p, t, k/ when they immediately precede a voiceless consonant (i.e. a consonant produced without vibration of the vocal chords). Thus *Bradford* is /brætfəd/ and *could swing* (l. 34) is /kʊtswɪŋ/.

6   /r/ is a flap (see p. 61).

7   /t/ when final may be realized as a glottal stop [ʔ] (e.g. *that* l. 43; see p. 62).

8   *–ing* is /ɪn/.

9   /h/ is generally absent.

10   *make* and *take* are /mɛk/ and /tɛk/ (l. 56).

The recording

The speaker is a man who has lived in Bradford all his life. His accent is quite marked, but notice the variable presence of /h/. He talks about his school-days and events in his youth.

– Did you ever have any teacher you were scared of or . . . you know, you couldn't stand?

Oh, yes, definitely . . . oh, aye . . . a Miss Ingham . . . and Mr Priestley, I was rather scared of him . . . you know, but . . . Miss
5   Ingham, when I was a kid, she . . . she always . . . to me she seemed rather vicious, you know . . . er . . . instead of . . . you know, she'd

knee you with her knee as she came round, you know, you were sat on
the chair . . . and she'd kick her knee into your back if she thought
. . . you know . . . and she was rather vicious, I used to think . . . thin
10 lipped . . . rather . . . oh, aye . . . used to frighten you . . . Priestley
was . . . he was all right w . . . I . . . I think I was scared of him,
really scared, you know, and when he came in . . . aah! I couldn't
think . . . I couldn't . . . he looked over the door sometimes . . . you
know . . . oh, deary me, over the glass partition, you know, in the
15 door . . . oh, he's coming in . . . and, honestly, I couldn't think when
he were in sometimes . . . especially if he took us in mental arith-
metic . . . oo, help . . . and when he took us in ear tests, that were as
bad, nearly . . . he'd tell you . . . he'd say sometimes, put two fingers
in your mouth . . . and, you know, he'd have you putting two fingers
20 in . . . three . . . four . . . five . . . put your foot in . . . aye, you know,
that sort of thing he'd make you open your mouth that way . . . I
mean, you couldn't sing with your teeth, he said, like that, you know
. . . you've got to open your mouth to sing . . . and he used to open
his . . . and he'd about two teeth in the middle . . . sort of thing, you
25 know, all of us kids, you know, looked and he seemed to have three or
four, you know, missing or more happen just two good . . . oh aye, he
were a lad, I tell you . . . certainly f . . . fri . . . well, I won't say,
frightened you, but you were frightened of him, you know . . . he . . .
he . . . er . . . oh dear . . . as I say, he used to put such a fear into me I
30 couldn't think . . . I remember that quite well . . . aye . . . oh wasn't I
glad when he went out . . .

Well one of the funniest ever . . . was when we were . . . playing on a
swing bridge, you know . . . and er . . . you were seeing how far you
could swing the bridge out . . . and then . . . it wasn't funny really
35 . . . the . . . but, you mean we laughed afterwards about it . . . on the
canal . . . it was swing . . . at t'swing bridge at Seven Arches . . .
swinging it out, you know, and you jump and see how far you can go
on it . . . and then one of them jumped into the canal, you see . . .
you see . . . but that didn't finish . . . you see we were . . . thought of
40 making . . . er . . . dry his clothes . . . so they made a fire . . . took
his clothes off, you see and . . . they couldn't get any . . . slow
burning stuff, it were all quick burning stuff, you see . . . and there
they were running round with bracken and things like that, making a
big fire, and one kid . . . holding his shirt, you see, up to t'fire, and it
45 caught fire . . . burnt his shirt . . . wasn't funny at the time, of
course, but it's funny when you tell it . . . you see . . . you think

about it, and things like that . . . oh, the things like that, you know, what you did as kids . . . aye . . . er . . . and you're in a field, like, and I remember my brother . . . we were caught redhanded in this field,
50 you know . . . what are you doing in here? Well, my brother just looked and says, what's up with you, he says, this is Farmer Budd's field . . . we had no idea who Farmer Budd were or not, you know, but this chap thought . . . he were er just . . . er . . . a chap that was keeping us out, you see . . . that were a funny incident, afterwards . . . it wasn't at the time . . . you know, our Clifford had just the presence of mind to say. . . make out that he knew the farmer, which we didn't . . .

Notes

1 Past tense of BE is *were* (l. 16) for all persons.
2 *You were sat there* (l. 7) = *You were sitting there. I was sat, I was stood* are widely used in parts of the north and west of England, rather than *I was sitting, I was standing.*
3 *he'd about* (l. 24). This is the full verb HAVE (see p. 20).
4 *the* may be /t/ (e.g. *to t'fire*, l. 44).
5 *always* (l. 5) is /ɔːləz/, a form found in other accents.
6 *kid* for *child* (l. 44) is colloquial and not restricted to any particular area.
7 *happen* (l. 26) = *perhaps.*

VII. Liverpool

The accent of Liverpool is limited to the city itself, to urban areas adjoining it, and to towns facing it across the River Mersey (although its influence may be detected in other neighbouring accents). While the accent is northern rather than southern in character, it differs in a number of ways from other northern urban varieties, including those of the rest of Lancashire, the county in which Liverpool stands. Some of the differences show the influence of the large numbers of Irish people, especially from southern Ireland, who have settled in Liverpool over the last hundred years.

1 The Liverpool accent is northern in that:
    (a) There is no contrast between pairs of words like *put* and *putt*, both being /put/ (WL 4, 5). There is no /ʌ/ vowel
    (b) /æ/ occurs in words like *dance*, *daft* etc., which in RP have /ɑː/ (see p. 56; WL 21–6).

Figure 5.12

(c) Words like *book* and *cook* have the vowel /uː/ (see p. 55; there are no examples on the tape).

2 Unlike in other northern urban accents (but in common with Newcastle), the final vowel of words like *city* and *seedy* is /iː/ (see p. 57).

3 There is no contrast in Liverpool speech between pairs of words like *fair* (RP /fɛə/) and *fir* (RP /fɜː/) (WL 34–7). The most typical realization of the vowel is [ɛː], but other forms, including [ɜː], are also heard.

4 (a) /p, t, k/ are heavily aspirated or even affricated (cf. cockney, p. 72). Thus:

can't (l. 5) [kxɑːnt]
straight (l. 12) [streɪts]
back (l. 18) [bakx]

In final position, /p, t, k/ may be realized as fricatives [ɸ s x].

(b) Related to this phenomenon is the relative infrequency of glottal stops in Liverpool speech.

(c) Between vowels, the first of which is short, /t/ may be realized as [ɾ]. This is limited to certain lexical items e.g. *matter*, *what*, *but*, *get* (e.g. l. 23, *got a job*: [ɡɒɾəjɒb]). This is a feature found in other parts of the north of England.

5 /r/ is usually a flap, [ɾ] (see p. 61) (e.g. *three*, l. 1; *real*, l. 3; *cigarettes*, l. 6).

6 /h/ is usually absent, but is sometimes present (e.g. l. 42, *him and her*).

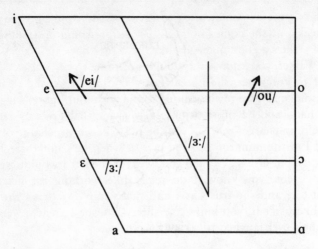

Figure 5.13 Typical realizations of certain Liverpool vowels

7   /ei/ and /ou/ are narrow diphthongs (WL 8, 40, 41 and WL 12, 38, 39) (figure 5.13).
8   Initially, /ð/ may be [d] (e.g. l. 11, *there*: [dɛ:]).
9   (a) The suffix *-ing* is /ɪn/.
    (b) Words like *singer* and *thing* (see p. 63) have [ŋg]. A clear example, because it precedes a vowel, is *thing*, l. 19.
10 All the features mentioned so far have covered particular segments of speech. But there is another feature, velarization, which is present throughout Liverpool speech and which gives it a distinctive quality. Velarization is the accompaniment of other articulations by the raising of the back of the tongue towards the soft palate (as in the production of dark /l/).

The recording

The speaker is a middle-aged barmaid who has lived all her life in Liverpool. She talks about pubs she knows, and people who work in them. The word list reader is younger and has a less pronounced accent.

Yeh, she's gone to America for three weeks, so we all go sad again next week . . . she comes over . . . I'll go polishing everything next week . . . she's a good manager, like, isn't she? but er . . . she's a real Annie Walker, you know, everything's got to be so . . . she's . . . once
5 you get to know her, she's great but you can't drink and you can't have a smoke . . . we're all walking round with four lighted cigarettes in our hand and having a drink off everyone that gives us one . . . yeh, we're in charge, yeh . . . well he's . . . he's er in charge of them all and I'm the monitor . . . I'm er . . . when he's not there I'm in
10 charge . . . but er it's . . . I tell you what, if she left I wouldn't go out there . . . cos, you know, I do really like working for her. She's straight . . . and she trusts you and that's imp . . . that's the main thing, like, isn't it, you know . . . she is . . . she's great . . . I don't think she's ever laughed till I went there . . .

15 Course as I say, when you do your work you don't need erm a boss, do you? that's what I say. . . this . . . this manager's made up . . . he said erm . . . he's never co . . . he'll give us the tills, then he comes back about four o'clock, and we've all locked up and gone . . . everything for him . . . he says, one thing about it, he says, I
20 haven't got to stand over yous . . . only the night time, you know . . . course, where it is, of a night they have a lot of er, you know, some that'll come a couple of nights, all these part-time students . . . and some of them . . . er . . . got a job . . . going to Spain and then want a few bob extra and then they just leave it. I don't know
25 whether they tap her till or what they do, but . . . he has to be there for them of a night time . . . yeh, but it is, it's er . . . and it's a pub that you wouldn't be frightened to bring anybody into, isn't it? . . . you know, it's beautiful . . . er yeh . . . true yeh . . . oh yeh, you say . . . I say bye-bye in there, I say tarrah up here . . .

30 Mind you, she'll be round there drunk now if you went into the Winifred for a drink . . . but I've never seen barmaids like them. They go round well away shouting and everything and . . . and the boss and the manageress is standing watching them . . . but they must be all right, kind of thing, or otherwise they wouldn't put up with it,
35 would they, like . . . true, yeh . . . well, this is it . . . mind you, there's been three man . . . three managers er sacked from there for bad takings . . . so they can't be er all that good . . . and two of them is two that's been through each . . . one that's, you know, er been sacked . . . yeh, that was [*name erased*] . . . but then, after that
40 there was erm a stout one named Jean . . . and John . . . she was

er an Australian, I think yeh, and she was here that long waiting for a
place that I took her in for three weeks . . . him and her . . . and they
were . . . she was a great person . . . I was made up because I didn't
take no rent off her, Stan, cos . . . I was . . . every hafpenny she had
45 had gone . . . paying for storage of furniture and she had dogs and
. . . all er so I just let her live here, like, but she used to have a
catering there as well, like Mrs Crighton. When I come home I'd have
a three course dinner, and I couldn't leave a handkerchief down it was
washed and ironed. I was made up because I didn't have to do
50 nothing to help her . . . but, anyhow, it . . . he finished up erm . . .
er . . . a night watchman on Runcorn bridge . . . that's the only place
she could get a house was Runcorn . . . but it was a shame, though,
with the money she had and she was in . . . born in New Zealand
and . . . everything and her staff pulled her right down . . . it is . . .
55 she said to me, she said, Bridie, she said, they didn't take it in
handfuls, they took it in fistfuls . . . and she was a real good
manager t . . . to them, you know, you know especially Christmas,
she wouldn't buy them er a box of handerkerchiefs, something like
that, it'd be a suit . . . or a dress . . . and buy all their children, but
60 yet they done all that on her like, you know, yeh . . . wouldn't be Mrs
Crighton . . . she'd only l . . . find her once and that would be your
lot, you'd be through the door.

Notes

1 There is multiple negation (see p. 22):
   I didn't take no rent off her (l. 44)
   I didn't have to do nothing to help her (l. 49)
2 (a) Past tense of COME = *come* (l. 47).
   (b) Past tense of DO = *done* (l. 60; see p. 25).
3 *yous* (/ju:z/ when stressed, and /jəz/ when not stressed) is plural *you*. It is
   a feature too of some Irish English.
4 The speaker makes a distinction between *bye-bye* and *tarrah*, both
   meaning *goodbye* (l. 29). She uses the former in settings which she
   regards as socially superior.
5 *Annie Walker* (l. 4) was a well known television character, the landlady
   of a pub, who was strict with her staff.
6 There are some perhaps unfamiliar lexical items:
       made up (l. 16) = very pleased
       tap (l. 25) = take money from
       well away (l. 32) = decidedly intoxicated
       where it is (l. 21) = the thing is
7 *like* (l. 3), *you know* (l. 4), *kind of thing* (l. 34) are best regarded as
   colloquialisms.

Figure 5.14

VIII. Edinburgh

The vowel systems of Scottish English accents are radically different from those of England, and it is therefore not so helpful to describe them in terms of differences from RP. Scottish Standard English speakers most usually have vowel systems approximately as given below (with words in which these vowels appear).

/i/	bee beer seedy meet meat			/u/	pull put boot poor
/e/	bay plate weight their mate	/ɪ/	pit bird fir city	/o/	pole boat board nose knows
/ɛ/	pet fern there	/ʌ/	putt fur	/ɔ/	cot caught paws pause paw pot Paul doll
		/a/	bard hat dance daft half father farther		
/ai/	buy	/au/	bout	/ɔi/	boy

It will be noted that:

1   Vowels such as RP /ɪə/, /ɜː/ do not occur. This is because Scottish accents have preserved post-vocalic /r/ (see p. 58), the loss of which in RP led to the development of these newer vowels. Pairs of words like *bee* and *beer* (WL 7, 14) thus have the same vowel, but are distinguished by the presence or absence of /r/. The /r/ is normally a flap (see p. 61) but may also be a frictionless continuant.

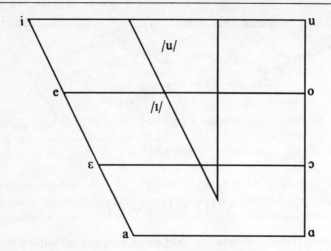

Figure 5.15 Typical realizations of certain Edinburgh vowels

2 Pairs of words such as *cot/caught* (WL 32, 33), *pull/pool* (WL 27, 28), *Pam/palm* are not distinguished (p. 57). Length is not generally a distinctive feature of Scottish vowels. Monophthongs are 'pure' – there is no trace of diphthongization.
3 For many Scottish speakers, words such as *fern, fur, fir* have different vowels. Different accents differ as to how far they preserve this distinction (WL 34, 35, 36).
4 A distinction is made between pairs of words like *tide: tied* (WL 46, 47), *booze: boos*, the second vowel in each case being longer. The basis for the distinction is that the second word in each pair has a word-final vowel plus an inflectional ending: *tie + d* (cf. London *pause: paws*, p. 71).
5 A distinction is made between pairs of words like *which* /hwɪč/ and witch /wɪč/. /hw/ is usually a single sound [ʍ], a voiceless [w].

The accent we have chosen to represent Scottish English comes from Edinburgh (except for the word list – see below). While there are considerable differences between Edinburgh speech and the speech of other Scottish cities, the accents are sufficiently similar to act as a good guide as to what to expect in Scotland in general. In listening to accents of Scottish English, the following points should also be noted.
1 /ɪ/ and /u/ may be central [ə] and [ʉ].
2 The glottal stop is a frequent realization of /t/ (see p. 62; *better*, l. 9; *that*, l. 11).

3 /h/ is present.
4 *–ing* is /ɪn/.

The recording

There are two main speakers on the tape. The word list reader is from Glasgow and is at present studying at an English University. Although her accent clearly identifies her as Scottish, it is by no means strong.

The second speaker is from Edinburgh, and his accent is rather stronger, (e.g. he has glottal stops representing /t/ between vowels. He talks about a certain area of Edinburgh as it was when he was young.

They were high tenement buildings and er many er sub-let houses, you know, broken up er bigger houses into . . . the room and kitchen was about the average house in these days, what we called the room and kitchen . . . with perhaps a toilet inside or outside on the
5 landings . . . but there was no such thing as bathrooms . . . in these days in these areas, you know? . . .

Adam Street, which was in the centre of that area there was some very very good houses, rather old-fashioned but quite good houses with fairly big rooms and that, and these were sort of better class
10 people er people with maybe . . . s . . . minor civil servants and things like that . . . you know, that had . . . be able to afford dearer rents and that in these days, you know. But the average working-class man . . . the wages were very small . . . the rents would run from anything from about five shillings to seven shillings, which was about
15 all they could have possibly afforded in these days . . . you just had to er . . . so it didnr . . . it didn re . . . matter how many a family you had . . . er if it was two rooms, well, Devil take the hindmost . . . aye, you couldn't get out of your environment, you see, you just had to suffer it and make the b . . . most of it . . . and they all survived,
20 that was the great thing . . . no . . . no . . . no I think they were better fed than these days, you know, the . . . they used to . . . the quality of the food was better, I think, and the meat . . . no, that's correct . . . it was er . . . pretty coarse meal and all that sort of thing and every-thing was much more er farm produce was much more naturally
25 grown, and things like that . . . so that . . . so there . . . there were very big families, you know, there . . . the average family was n . . . nothing under five children in a family . . . very very rarely . . . oh

you'd have them anything up to nines, nine in a family living in two
rooms, there was no segregation or anything like that. The only hope
30 was that somebody would get married or something like that, you
know . . .

There were some great stories in that area, you know, there were
some really . . . people were . . . they were quite er amusing that er
how they overcame their difficulties, you know, with er . . . they could
35 improvise . . . er . . . I remember a very funny thing though I don't, I
was quite young at the time, but there was a place in the Pleasance,
off the Pleasance, called the Oakfield Court, and it was a very very
rough quarter, everybody fought with each other in . . . in circulation
. . . er one fought one one week or the other . . . it was just drink and
40 a fight, you know, er very clean fighting . . . that er when they got into
a good mood, they had what they called the party called the
surpriser! . . . and they . . . somebody took the bed down in one of
the houses and er moved the furniture out into the street and all that,
and they got two or three bottles of beer and had a party, and . . . er
45 . . . they were very lucky if it lasted t . . . er the fight started again
. . .

Notes

1   *with* is consistently /wɪ/. In more prestigious Scottish speech, *with* is
/wɪθ/ rather than /wɪð/.
2   *this* and *these* with time reference may be found in Scottish English
where *that* and *those* are used in standard English English (l. 3).

IX. Belfast

In the northern part of Northern Ireland speech is quite similar to
that of Scotland, which is where large numbers of settlers to Ulster
came from. In the south of the province, on the other hand, speech
derived originally from that of the West Midlands and the south-west
of England. Belfast speech combines features from both north and
south.

1   As in Scotland, there is post-vocalic /r/ (see p. 58). /r/ is realized as
a retroflex, frictionless continuant [ɹ] (see p. 61). It is similar to
word-initial /r/ in RP, except that the tip of the tongue is pulled
back somewhat further.

Figure 5.16

2 (a) The vowel system is similar to that of Scottish accents:

/i/	bee beer seedy meet meat			/u/	put boot pull pool poor	
/e/	bay bear plate weight mate	/ɪ/	pit fir bird city fern fur	/o/	boat board pole knows nose pour pore	
/ɛ/	pet	/ʌ/	putt	/ɔ:/	Paul paw doll pause caught	
		/a/	pat bard hat dance daft half father farther	/ɒ/	cot	
/ai/	buy tide tied	/au/	bout	/ɔi/	boy	

(b) Vowels are short before /p, t, k, č/, long before other consonants or when final.

(c) In Belfast speech the actual realization of a vowel may vary considerably according to the sound which follows it. For example, /a/ in *daft* has a realization not very different from

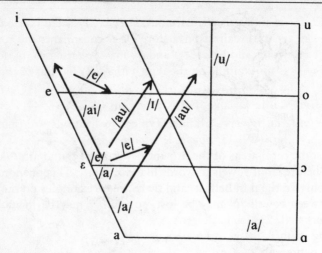

Figure 5.17 Typical realizations of certain vowels in Belfast speech

/ɑ:/ in RP, while in *bag* it may be [ɛ] (figure 5.17). Since the vowel in *beg* may also be [ɛ], the two words may not always be distinguished. This raises the question of whether it would be better to consider the vowel in *bag* to be /ɛ/ rather than /a/. For various reasons we have chosen not to do this, but the reader should be aware that the analysis of vowels could have been somewhat different from the one we propose (cf. /e/ v /ɛ/, and /o/ v /ɔ:/).

(d) The following notes on vowels should be read in association with figure 5.17:

  (i) /u/ is central, [ʉ]

  (ii) /e/ is normally realized as a diphthong varying between [ɛə] and [iə], but in words like *bay* (WL 8] and *say* (l. 12) the vowel is a monophthong, [ɛ]. In plural and possessive forms of these words, too, the vowel is [ɛ] (e.g. *days*, l. 50), and *days* therefore contrasts with *daze*

  (iii) /ɪ/ is fairly central, [ɨ]. Although *fir*, *fur*, *fern* and *fair* may sometimes have different vowels, they all tend to be pronounced with [əɨ] which is probably best analysed as /ɪr/

  (iv) /ɔ:/ and /ɒ/ contrast only before /p, t, k/, as in *caught* and *cot* (WL 32, 33)

  (v) As has been mentioned above, realizations of /a/ may vary considerably. Before certain consonants (e.g. /f/ and

/s/ in *daft*, WL 23, and *class*, l. 21) there is a back or central realization. Before other consonants the vowel is front, and before /g/ and /ŋ/ may be raised to [ɛ]. (There is no example on the tape with /g/ or /ŋ/, but *back*, l. 10, is [bæk])

(vi) /ai/ is variable, but is often [ɛɪ] (WL 9, 46, 47)

(vii) /ɑu/ is very variable. Typical realizations are [æʉ] and [ɛi] (WL 13; *house*, l. 1; *down*, l. 6).

3   In some rural areas of the province, /j/ may be found after /k/ and /g/ before front vowels in words like *car*, [kjaɹ]. This phenomenon is only vestigial in Belfast, and there are no examples on the tape.

4   Between vowels /ð/ may be lost, so *mother* may be [mɔ̈ːəɹ] and *another* (l. 23) [ənɔ̈ːəɹ].

5   *–ing* is /ɪn/.

6   /h/ is present.

7   Certain words which have /ʊ/ in RP and other accents may have /ʌ/ in Belfast speech: e.g. *wood* may be pronounced [wʊd] or [wʌd].

The recording

The main speaker is a middle-aged woman with a distinctive Belfast accent. The man who asks her questions is younger, and his accent is less broad. The woman talks about her past and about the fighting in the city.

. . . born in this house . . . and still in it . . . Raymond

– You were born in this house?

I was born in this house, yes . . . b . . .

– So then you haven't lived in any other parts of Belfast, just this
5   part. Oh aye . . . when I was about eight years of age my mother went down to the Ormeau Road to live, in Parscoe Street. But then . . . you see my Uncle Tommie's lived here, and his wife died . . . and he got married again, my mother come back to my granny . . . her . . . er . . . mother and we've been there ever since again, that was in
10   . . . during the . . . the war, 1941 or something we come back here, you know. So, counting all round, we weren't so long on the Ormeau Road, really, you know. I'd say about ten years, maybe twelve years, you know, no longer.

– And where have you worked in Belfast? What different places?

15 Well that's the only place I've ever worked in, Raymond.

– In where?

Oh, aye, when I come out . . . when I was a wee girl of fourteen I worked in a . . . in a boot repairer's shop . . . they sold shoes and stuff too, but mostly repair work they done. Well I stuck it for a
20 couple . . . for a year or so, and then, when I was about sixteen or so, my grandmother got me into a place called Carsons, a very high class bakery shop, opposite the City Hall . . . that's gone, like, completely now, but . . . I done another couple of years there, then they closed up, there were two old sisters owned it really, you know, they were
25 coming up to retirement age, really, and they . . . they sold their business then, you see, so . . . I wasn't out of work that long until another lady got me into Inglis's . . .

– But, wh . . . when the sort of troubles were at their height recently, there was a lot of gunfighting around that area . . .

30 Oh there was

– Now could you . . . was there any time when you yourself were sort of . . . er . . . in danger around there . . . when you had any . . . can you remember any time when . . . you were frightened.

Well I wouldn't say in danger, really, Rust . . . er . . . Raymond . . .
35 we heard shooting and all going on when we were in work, you know. W . . . we had a window just looked out on to Eliza Street . . . and our cloakroom, as we call it . . . when we used to hear the gunfire we used to look out . . . which is a very dangerous thing to do really, you know. Well then they had a gun battle . . . Belvoir . . . at the time of
40 the Internment . . . remember the time of Internment . . . there was trouble down there really, you know, and . . . er . . . they'd lifted some people that . . . old people and all, like old men that they had a grudge against that they should'nt have lifted really, you know what I mean? And . . . er . . . it was just stonethrowing and troops and one
45 thing and another, and a bit of . . . it went on all day. Well then there was a gun battle started on top of Inglis's . . . it's a flat roof Inglis's.

– And you were working in the place at the time?

No we were . . . funny enough, we were o . . . I was off on a week's holiday. . . then when Internment started, you know . . . but . . . em

50 . . . I think they had to close up for a couple of days, really, you know, until it died down but there was a fellow, one of the terrorists was shot on the roof, really, you know . . .

– Yeh, did you know any of the people that you knew in Inglis's who . . . sort of . . . were shot or anything like that or had er . . .

55 No, only just round about that didn't work at Inglis's, really, you know, the time the Republican er . . . remember the time they had a . . . a bit of a feud between the two sides. Republican and the . . .

– The Provisionals?

Aye . . . it was the Provisionals and another . . . with Bernadette
60 Devlin was over . . . now there was . . . the initials, I just can't remember, the initials, you know what I mean, Social something, you know . . . just forget what the initials . . . well they had a bit of a go at each other, you see, and there was shooting and . . . I remember one time when I was in work at that time . . . and erm . . . everybody
65 was lying low at the time, you know, I mean they all disappearing . . . I think half of Inglis's disappeared for a few days, even the security man disappeared . . . they were all went . . . aye . . . y'know and then in a few days time when it was all over they all come trotting back again . . . you know, you don't know who . . . who was who, you
70 know what I mean.

– But were you never afraid, like, in the middle of winter going down there . . . an . . . you walked down there, didn't you? It must have been dark in the early mornings or evenings coming back . . . it's a dangerous place to go now at night, isn't it . . . I mean some people
75 wouldn't want to go there.

Yes, I know, well . . . I never thought of danger, really, you know what I mean, it never struck me . . . you know.

– I mean, some people wouldn't walk in that area.

That's right, I know . . . I remember one day there was shooting all
80 round over something, I don't know what it was . . . oh . . . down all the streets there was shots getting fired here, there and everywhere . . . and at about five o'clock I was coming home and it was pretty sh . . . pretty dark, you know, and I saw this yellow car sitting up Cromac Street, and a fellow over the bonnet of it . . . I said that's very like Harry Short's, you know, anyway when I got up it was Harry Short . . . and all the shooting was going round him . . . and

there was Harry, his car or something had went wrong and he was
. . . says I, Harry what are you doing here, says I, you could be shot,
says I, you're . . . leaning over your bonnet fixing your car . . .

90   – What did he say to that?

He laughed hearty at the idea . . . well he had to get a tow home by
the RAC . . . something went wrong where he couldn't start his car
. . . he seemed to be . . . he didn't know that the shooting was going
around him, he was that interested in his car getting started . . .

Notes

1   (a) *come* (l. 8, 10, 17, 68) is the past tense of COME (see p. 24).
    (b) *done* (l. 19, 23) is the past tense of DO (see p. 25).
    (c) *went* (l. 67) is the past participle of GO (see p. 24).
2   *says I* (l. 88), see p. 26.
3   *hearty* (l. 91), see p. 29.

X. Dublin

Although there are similarities between the English of the northern
and southern parts of Ireland – /l/ is clear [l] in all positions
throughout Ireland, for instance – the accents of Belfast and Dublin
are very different. One reason for this is that there was no Scottish
influence on the development of Dublin English.

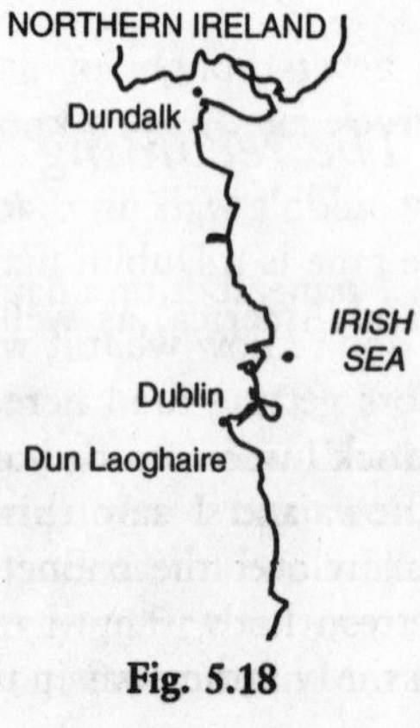

Fig. 5.18

1   In some respects, the English of the Republic of Ireland, except that of the far north, resembles that of Bristol and other parts of south-west England. For instance, post-vocalic /r/ (see p. 58) occurs, and the RP vowels /ɪə/, ɛə/ and /ʊə/ are therefore absent.

2   /æ/, pronounced [a], and /ɑ:/, pronounced [a:], are distinct and are distributed much as in RP. Note /æ/ in *matter* (l. 23) and /ɑ:/ in *after* (l. 20). In other parts of Ireland, however, /æ/ and /ɑ:/ may not be distinct.

3   /ɒ/ is pronounced [ɑ], cf. *lot* (l. 21) and /ɔ:/ is pronounced [ɑ:].

4   /ai/ has a back first element [ɑɪ~ɒɪ] which is nevertheless distinct from /ɔi/, e.g. *while* (l. 35).

5   /ei/ and /ou/ are mostly monophthongs or narrow diphthongs.

6   There is a strong tendency for /ʊ/ and /ʌ/ not to be distinct in strongly local Dublin accents, e.g. /ʊ/ in *government* (l. 9), but /ʌ/ does occur, particularly in more educated speech.

7   /ɜ:/ does not occur in lower-status accents. Instead, as in Scottish English (p. 97), words such as *firm* (l. 3) have /ɪr/, words such as *Germans* (l. 29) have /ɛr/, and words such as *work* (l. 2) have /ʊ/.

8   Irish English has /æ/ rather than /ɛ/ in *any, anyone*, cf. *anyone* (l. 16).

9   /θ/ and /ð/ are often pronounced not as fricatives but as dental stops [t̪] and [d̪]. Before /r/, /t/ and /d/ may also be pronounced as dental stops, so there may be no distinction /t̪r/ – /tr/, /d̪r/ – /dr/, e.g. *true/through* [t̪ru:]. Note dental stops on the recording in *third* (l. 11), *north* (l. 15), and elsewhere.

10 /h/ is normally pronounced.

11 /p, t, k/ tend to be strongly aspirated, e.g. *it* (l. 46).

The recording

The main speaker on the tape is a Dublin man who is talking about experiences in Canada and America, as well as early 19th-century Irish history.

They controlled the painters' union, so they eventually after a short while they got me into the painters' union and I did clerical work. I was a trainee manager in Ireland for an English firm from London, State Express 335 cigarettes, that's where I met my wife. I was her
5   boss and I'm still her boss. My father was in the RAF, so through his

. . . and he was also in the First World's War, and I also lived in a British ex-service house in Bray in County Wicklow. My mother and father did, so the thing there is that . . . when I came down from Canada I was working for the Canadian government, in a clerical
10 position, but I had two daughters and my wife was pregnant with the third and the clerical job was paying $80 a week and the painting trade was paying $134 a week, so obviously I don't have to tell you what happened. So I went to night school and I had some Irish Americans, they were Irish-Scotch Americans, the mother from
15 Glasgow, the father from the north of Ireland. Well, the Finnegan family taught me the greatest apprenticeship that anyone could ever got. I got a great apprenticeship off the Finnegans and unfortunately for them, luckily for me, because of my background in, in management, and being able to read blueprints, and estimate, I became the
20 superintendent. So I was their boss after six months.

I played a lot of that Gaelic football, the Irish football, for years and I was also a soccer player, and I'd been involved in many, many organisations. As a matter of fact, as Mary says, that . . . we have a, an Easter Sunday commemoration mass here in the centre that I
25 run on my own every year. And, they, the last two years now they done a video tape on it. And then there was a, we give about a bo . . . twenty, twenty-five minute tribute to the leaders of 1916. That's when, you know, that they rose up against England at the, at the encouragement of the Germans. Now, my father was in the Dardanelles
30 when that happened. So, the thing was that a lot of, a lot of people in Ireland during that period, there was a lot killed in Ireland in all factories and firms. They just locked the doors. No s–, they were trying to union organize and they just locked them out. And most of the children at that time had to be sent to England to fellow union
35 members to, to feed 'em, and keep them, while this happened. And, and actually the First World's War started in 1914, and England were giving a bonus. They were stationed all over Ireland at that time. They were giving a bonus to anyone that volunteered. Well my father volunteered in 1915, fifteen years old, he was born in 1900. And the
40 biggest mistake England made was Lloyd George sending as they called them the Black and Tan. Now that was like the veterans of Vietnam. They were the veterans of the First World's War who come back where unemployment, the economy was bad, and half of these people ended up in gaol. Well, what they did, what Lloyd George did,

45 instead of letting the regular army quell that, they sent these people
over in 1920, in a, in a vigilante uniform as they say it in Ireland.

Notes

1 *First World's War* (l. 6): more usually *First World War.*
2 *could ever got* (l. 16) = *could ever've got.*
3 *off* (l. 17) = Standard English *from.*
4 *they done* (l. 26) = Standard English *did.*
5 *Lloyd George* (l. 40): Prime Minister of Great Britain 1916–22.
6 *come* (l. 42) = Standard English *came.*

XI. Devon

We conclude this section of the book with an examination of three
Traditional Dialects of English which are very different from Standard English and RP (see. p. 30). Varieties of this type are much less
likely to be encountered by non-native learners, but are nevertheless
of considerable interest.

The first traditional dialect is that of a rural area of Devon, in the
south-west of England. The accent of this area is reasonably similar
to that of Bristol, but there are some very clear differences.

Fig. 5.19

1 Devon lacks Long Mid Diphthonging, so that /ei/ = [e:], e.g. *face*
(l. 2), and /ou/ = [o:] or [u:], e.g. *local* (l. 3).
2 /u:/ is a front vowel approaching [y:] e.g. *improve* (l. 45).
3 At the beginning of words, RP /f, θ, s, š/ may be /v, ð, z, ž/ e.g.
scythe /zai/ (l. 17), *see* /zi:/ (l. 22), *thing* /ðiŋ/ (l. 37).

4   As far as grammar is concerned, the following can be noted:

(a)   the present tense of the verb *to be* is *be* for all persons (see p. 32) e.g. *ponies be* (l. 28)

(b)   *Isn't* and *wasn't* are pronounced *idden* and *wadden*, e.g. *isn't* (l. 21)

(c)   The pronoun system is as discussed in Chapter 2, p. 32. *He* is used for count nouns, including female animals: *he's a yow* (l. 9), *he got to* (l. 5). The object form of *he* is *'en: when you zee 'en* (l. 22). Object forms may be used where subject forms would be expected: *us would call 'em* (l. 1), *wadd 'em* [= what do they] (l. 36). Subject forms may be used where object forms would be expected: *from they* (l. 32)

(d)   (i)   *seed* = saw

(ii)   *tis* = it's

The recording

The speaker on the recording is a farmer in his fifties, talking about various aspects of farming and rural life.

Now there's some Scotch black-face sheep, that is. Us would call 'em possibly yows, or a ram, but that's Scotch black-face. That idden a local breeds. No. Now the local breeds, you see, there was the Widecombe white-face. Now, Widecombe white-face was a, is a
5   curly-coated sheep and he, he got, he got horns, the ram carries horns, but the yow don't, and that was very much a local breed that was sold here at Widecombe Fair each year. Then there's the grey-face Dartmoor. Now the grey-face Dartmoor haven't got no horns, whether he's a ram, or whether he's a yow, a bigger sheep
10   than the white-face, still big heavy curly coat, something like a Devon long-wool, but this was brought in, these here Scotch sheep was brought down to, to Dartmoor . . . oh beggar . . . oh back, fifty years ago I suppose. So, very much a breed here on the moors now. And there's a lot of fuzz there in the pictures, idden there? Lot of
15   fuzz, idden it? Beggar me, there idden a lot of grass there . . . enough grass to starve a rabbit, look like it!

That's a zy, yes, now that's a zy, and the interesting thing is that that is a manufactured snead. Now all zies got a snead . . . snead's the handle! . . . snead's the handle, and years ago you used to cut a snead
20   if you seed the right-sized, the right-shaped stick, you see, and there is a Devonshire saying is 'When is the right time to cut a shovel-

stick?' And th' answer is 'When you zee 'en!' So, so, you, it's the same
with a snead. He got to have a, he got to have the right curve in it,
see. No, no, generally halse, generally halse or ash, generally, yeah. I
25 should think that's ash, but generally halse or ash. Because it tends to
grow, but the right way with not too many natches in it. You don't
want too many natches in it.

No, proper Dartmoor ponies be either a nice sort of dark, bit darker
than chestnut, see, or black, but this here stuff, see, tis, that idden,
30 that idden proper Dartmoor ponies. National Park . . . they've got a
sort of scheme going now, I believe, that with a little bit of sort of
encouragement, trying to keep people to sort of stop breeding from
they, see, but breed from the proper Dartmoor ponies, and, and the
Dartmoor ponies be hardier than those ponies, see, and that's why
35 years ago you didn't get half the trouble with these here Dartmoor
. . . whadd 'em call 'em . . . the Pony Protection Society, and that
sort of thing. Kicking up a shindig about the fact that the ponies be
up a-starving on the moor, because the true Dartmoor pony, he was
hardy, hardy see, he could weather the weather and us used to get
40 worst winters then than us do now, but he would, he would bide up
on the moors. And he'd dig away the snow, see, and get at the fuzz
bushes and th' heather and eat grass in under the fuzz bushes and
he'd live happy, happy as Larry. And then, course, when it got that
riding ponies was all the craze, they started breeding in this sort of
45 stuff and trying to sort of improve 'em a bit. You get piebalds, 'cause
they like, the kiddies like the piebalds, and the screwballs, and that
sort of . . . but, no, ponies, yeah.

Notes

1 *yows* (l. 2) = ewes.
2 *fuzz* (l. 13) = furze (gorse).
3 *zy* (l. 17) = scythe.
4 *zee* (l. 22) = see.
5 *halse* (l. 24) = hazel.
6 *natch* (l. 26) = notch.
7 *shindig* (l. 37) = fuss.
8 *bide* (l. 40) = stay.

XII. Northumberland

The speech of Northumberland is represented here by a traditional dialect speaker from Tyneside, the urban area which dominates this region. Northumbrian speech is similar in some respects to that of Scotland.

1 (a) As in other northern English accents, pairs of words like *put* and *putt* are not distinguished, /ʊ/ occurring in both (see p. 54). But:

(b) The final vowel in words like *city* and *seedy* is /iː/ see p. 57).

(c) As has been seen, /ei/ and /ou/ are wide diphthongs in the south of England, narrow diphthongs further north, and monophthongs in northern Lancashire and Yorkshire. On Tyneside they may be either monophthongs, [eː] and [oː] or opening diphthongs, [ɪe] and [uo]. But notice that *roll* (l. 62) has [ɔu].

2 (a) Again as in other northern accents, words like *dance* and *daft* have /æ/ (WL 22, 23).

Figure 5.20

(b) Words like farm and car have /ɑ:/.

(c) Words which have /ɔ:/ in RP are divided into two sets in Tyneside speech.

    (i) Those which have *al* in the spelling have /a:/ e.g. *talking* (l. 59), *called* (l. 12), *all* (l. 56).

    (ii) Those which do not have *al* in the spelling have /ɔ:/, as in RP (WL 18, 33, 44, 45; *morning* (l. 18).

(d) Words which have /ɜ:/ in RP have /ɔ:/ in a broad Tyneside accent. So, *first* (l. 10) and *shirt* (l. 34) are /fɔ:st/ and šɔ:t/, homonyms of *forced* and *short*.

By comparison with RP, the accent of Tyneside lacks one vowel, /ɜ:/, but has one extra, /a:/. Correspondences between the pure vowels we have mentioned can be represented as follows:

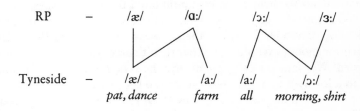

RP	–	/æ/	/ɑ:/		/ɔ:/	/ɜ:/
Tyneside	–	/æ/	/a:/	/a:/		/ɔ:/
		pat, dance	*farm*	*all*		*morning, shirt*

3 (a) Word final *-er(s)* or *-or(s)* is [ɐ(z)] (*tanner*, l. 4).

  (b) /ɪə/ is [iɐ] (WL 14; *here* (l. 3)).

  (c) /ʊə/ is [uɐ] (WL 42).

4 /ai/ is [ɛi] (*right* (l. 48).

5 /l/ is clear in all environments (WL 27–31).

6 /h/ is generally present.

7 *-ing* is /ɪn/ (*shilling*, l. 2).

8 Between vowels, /p, t, k/ are accompanied by a glottal stop. *city* is [sɪʔi:]; *happy* (l. 30) is [haʔi:] (see p. 62).

9 (a) Words which in RP have /aʊ/ may have /u:/ e.g. *about* (l. 4), *out* (l. 6).

  (b) (i) *knows* is /na:z/ (see l. 33 for contrast with *nose*); *though* is /ða:/ (l. 40).

     (ii) *was*, when stressed, is /wæz/; *what* is /wæt/; *who* (l. 67) is /we/.

     (iii) *no, do* (l. 29), *nobody* (l. 67) have /e/.

     (iv) *long* (l. 61) is /læŋ/.

     (v) *father* (l. 68) is [fæðɐ].

10 In parts of Northumberland and Durham /r/ may be uvular (the production of the sound involving tongue and uvula, rather than tongue and alveolar ridge). The recorded speaker's /r/ is variable. An example of uvular /r/ is found in *remember* (l. 11) (see p. 61).

The recording

The speaker is a man of about fifty who has lived almost all of his life in and around Newcastle. His accent is quite strong. He talks about the old days.

I'll tell you what, I often tell it at work. You know, they'd say to you, 'Hey, Jimmy, lend us a shilling, man'. What? Lend us a shilling . . . me and I'd say to them come here a minute I'll tell you. I says, I can remember when I used to shove a bairn about in a pram for a tanner a
5 week. Lot of money a tanner then a week. And I says, I've been pushed for money ever since, so they divn't come back. Put them out the road. Wey lad, get away, go on. Aye, he says, for a tanner. By, you can do a lot with a tanner. You can gan to the pictures, get yoursel a penny fish and a haipeth of chips, by God, yeh, and maybes a packet
10 of Woodbines for tuppence, and a match in, for to get your first smoke . . . bah . . . I once ge . . . remember getting some Cock Robins, called them Cock Robins, bah . . . they cock-robinned me, I'll tell you. I was at Newburn Bridge . . . that's it . . . you can see Newburn, it's across there and I was smoking away, faking, you
15 know, instead of just going ph ph . . . swallowing down, you know, I was sick and turned dizzy. I didn't know what hit us with these Cock Robins . . . bah, but they they were good ones . . .

This old woman says to me one morning . . . Sonny . . . Sonny, why you never said sonny them days you know. She says, would you like to
20 run a message for Mr Penn and for me. I says, yes I will do. She says, go up to the shop and get him an ounce of tobacco. Oh, I says, thank you very much, so I gans twaddling up the shop. When I gans back she give us thruppence, mind thruppence, you know, that's about forty, forty-two year ago, you know, Reg. Thruppence then was a lot
25 of money. I was there every day knocking at the door to see if she wanted any more messages. Aye thruppence. Wey lad, ay, I'm getting thruppence off that woman. What for? Wey, getting some baccy. Well, lad . . . Thruppence? What a lot of money that was. Oh dear me, oh, we used to do such things then, y . . .

30 We used to do some queer things then, but we were happy, man, aye,
we were happy. Once a rag man says to me . . . Hey sonny. . . What?
. . . He says, your hanky's hanging out . . . hanky. . . wey, you never
had a hanky then. You used to wipe your nose like that, you know. It
was my shirt tail hanging out of a hole in my pants . . . aye he says
35 . . . your hanky's hanging out. Well you never had a hanky then. Bah
. . . you used to gan to school. They used to line you up at school
there. You want a pair of shoes, I think. You want a pair of shoes.
Wey, you never seen them, you know, it was just a day out from
Durham County for somebody from Durham down the road. Them
40 were the days, though . . .

Then I went from there . . . and there's a house up there just beside
those two wireless poles. I went from there to there, and then I went
and got married and went and lived in with Florrie, and er I was like
a bit gypsy, I was in Blaydon first and Greenside I was, in Blaydon and
45 Greenside. That's what the doctor says. He says, Jimmy, you've a
little bit gypsy in you. He says we divn't know where you live. Then I
shifted from there to Crawcrook and from Crawcrook to Blaydon,
aye, that's right, aye . . . we sold the house at Crawcrook and I went
to Coventry, and when I come back I stopped with Florrie, and then I
50 got a council house into here. I've been in here about twelve year in.
Oh, if I gan out here I gan out with a stick, George, a stick in a big
box, that'd not be very long would it the box, about five foot ten, that
the measurement of us. When I get stiff, when I gan stiff about five
foot ten . . .

55 But you used to get summers, didn't you. Wey, you used to get the
winters and all, pet. Oh, dear me, ow the winters. You couldn't stand
the winters now. . . yous lot couldn't stand it, could they? Course we
used to get the grub, you know. There was a fellow . . . there was a
fellow at er . . . when I'm talking about grub . . . he used to make
60 leek puddings, you've heard of leek puddings, you know . . . but he
used to make them about a yard lang, see, and put the leek in, and
roll the leek up, see, just like er a sausage, see . . . and this fellow was
sitting, Japer Newton they called him, he had about four sons and a
lass, like, and he was sitting at the end of the table, like . . . all sitting
65 with our tongues hanging out, you know, George. He was sitting at
the end with a s . . . a big leek pudding. He says, er, who wants the
end? So nobody spoke, see, so he says again, who wants the end, you
buggers; Ted says I'll have the end, father, so he cut the bugger in

70 two. Aye, he cut it in two, a great big leek pudding about a yard lang, cut it in two . . .

Notes

l. 2 *us* = me (also l. 16).

l. 3 *I says* see p. 24.

l. 4 *bairn* = child (in Scotland too).

l. 4 *tanner* = six (old) pence (not limited to Tyneside).

l. 5 *I've been pushed for money:* I've been short of money.

l. 6 *divn't* = didn't, don't, or doesn't.

l. 7 *Wey:* exclamation common on Tyneside.

l. 8 *gan* = go (also l. 36).

l. 9 *a haipeth:* a half pennyworth (not limited to Tyneside).

l. 9 *maybes:* maybe.

Woodbines: once a common and inexpensive brand of cigarettes.

l. 10 *for to* = to (also found in Scottish and Irish English.)

Bah!: exclamation not limited to Tyneside.

l. 18 Note the two pronunciations of *sonny,* the first being an imitation of the woman's accent, which he clearly thinks was 'posh', RP or something approaching it.

l. 19 *Them* is used as demonstrative adjective.

l. 23 *give* as past tense of GIVE (see p. 24).

l. 23 *thruppence* = three pence (not limited to Tyneside).

l. 27 *baccy:* colloquial form for tobacco.

l. 32 *hanky:* colloquial form for handkerchief.

l. 38 *seen* as past tense of SEE (see p. 24).

l. 39 *Durham County* = Durham County Council.

l. 39 *Them* as demonstrative pronoun (see p. 29).

l. 49 *come* as past tense of COME (see p. 24).

l. 50 *twelve year* (see p. 30).

l. 56 *pet:* term of endearment much used on Tyneside.

l. 57 *yous* = you (cf. Liverpool, p. 96).

l. 58 *grub* (colloquial) = food.

l. 64 *lass* (northern and Scottish): girl.

l. 68 *bugger:* term of (often friendly) abuse, common in most parts of Britain. But also a 'taboo' word.

l. 68 *bugger* here refers to the pudding.

XIII. Lowland Scots

Of all the varieties of English spoken in the British Isles, these are probably the most unlike Standard English and RP. However, in this section we confine ourselves to urban varieties (Edinburgh and Glasgow). Rural varieties, which are spoken by a much smaller number of speakers, are even more different and therefore provide even greater difficulties for foreign learners.

As we have already seen, the vowel systems of all varieties of Scottish English are radically different from those of England (see section VIII). The traditional dialects spoken by urban working-class Lowland Scots speakers on our recordings, however, have the following additional features:

1 /u/ may often occur where RP has /au/: *house*, for instance, may be /hus/ = [hʉs], and is often written as *hoose* in Lowland Scots dialect literature, e.g. *round about* (l. 34).

2 Instead of having *coat* /kot/, *cot, caught* /kɔt/ as described in section VIII, working-class Edinburgh and Glasgow speakers may have *coat, cot* /kot/, *caught* /kɔt/. That is, pairs like *socks* and *soaks, clock* and *cloak* may be identical, e.g. *brought* (l. 31).

3 A number of words, which have /oʊ/ in RP and /o/ in Standard Scottish English have /e/ in Lowland Scots. Thus *home* is /hem/, *bone* is /ben/, *stone* is /sten/ and *no* is /ne/. This is often reflected in Lowland Scots dialect writing by spellings such as *hame* and *nae*. The same vowel also occurs in *do* /de/ and *to* /te/. Examples are *stones* /stenz/ (l. 29) and *going to* /gone/ (l. 38).

4 Many words, such as *arm, grass*, may have /ɛ/ rather than /a/: /ɛrm/, /grɛs/. Examples on the tape are *harm* (l. 39), *married* (l. 47).

5 Words such as *long, strong* have /a/ rather than /ɔ/ (cf. section XII), e.g. *wrong* /raŋ/.

6 In the west of Scotland, including Glasgow, words such as *land* can have /ɔ/ rather than /a/, e.g. *handy* (l. 44).

7 Past participles of verbs typically end in /t/ where Standard English would have /d/, e.g. *married* (l. 47), *feared* (l. 42).

The recording

There are two speakers on the tape. The first is an Edinburgh schoolboy talking about gang fighting. The second is an older Glasgow woman talking about her youth.

Yes . . . aw it's the gangs . . . they just fight with knives and bottles and big sticks . . . and bricks . . . takes place over at the big railway

over there . . . yes . . . they've got a gang . . . they call it Young
Niddrie Terror . . . round here they call it Young Bingham Cumbie
5   . . . and that's how it starts . . . they start fighting . . . yes . . . and
they fight with other yins, they fight with . . . Magdalene . . . that's
away along the main road there . . . if . . . Magdalene's just down
that road . . . yes . . . and they fight with the Northfields . . . and
they go away on buses . . . and go to a lot of other places . . . to fight
10   . . . aw . . . about sixteen and that . . . yes . . . yes . . . don't know
. . . no . . . yes . . . well . . . there's only one person that lives round
here . . . this part . . . and the rest are . . . some of them live away up
the road there . . . and they're all round the scheme . . . well . . .
there's one of them . . . he . . . he takes a lot of them on, he's right
15   strong . . . aye . . . well, they . . . they have nicknames . . . I forget his
name but . . . his nickname but . . . he is strong . . . he fights with all
these others . . . he takes about three on at a time . . . yes . . . yes . . .
because he is big . . . aw, the police come rou . . . round just . . . just
when it starts . . . see all the police at night, they're going round the
20   scheme . . . making sure there's no fights . . . and all the laddies just
run away when they see the police coming . . . yes . . . aye . . . they
run away and hide . . . till they think it's safe . . . not always . . . they
take them away down to the police station . . . well, if there's any
serious . . . injuries on anybody . . . they'll get put in the children's
25   home or that . . . so if they're old enough they'll get put there . . . no
. . . only one person . . . that was Billy . . . he was caught . . . just a
couple of nights or so ago . . . yes . . . some of them . . . some . . .
aw, they usually . . . there's wee-er laddies than me that goes round
there and start tossing stones at the laddies round there. They usually
30   get battered fae them if they get caught.

You don't know the way I was brought up. When I think on it now
. . . I think that it was kind of strict . . . because er . . . it was an
awful . . . oh a terrible lot of them living yet, and they're in the flats
and they're all round about, they've been meeting me with 'Bella, you
35   never . . . got doing what we did'. And yet we were happy. We were
quite happy in the house with my mother and father. And we were
sitting in that room with the wee screens, keeking out at them all
playing, in the summer at nine o'clock. We were gone to our bed.
Never done us any harm. Now, I think it's right, to be like that. And
40   we'd to ask my father if, if we'd a boyfriend, we'd to ask my father.
He would've died. I went with *him* for a year afore we got engaged.
And I went for other five year . . . I was feared to tell my father. My

mother said 'Belle, you need to tell your father'. I says 'You know what he is'. 'Cause I was handy, I was the last lassie, you know, and I
45 done everything. She says 'You'll need to tell him', I says 'No'. But Willy's mother . . . he was er . . . the youngest, and, ach, there were years atween the one next to him, they were all married, and she was a widow, and . . . I think they only got ten shillings then for a widow's pension. Oh, she would be awful old the now. So we just
50 made it up that we would stay single like that the now. 'You help your mother, and I'll help mine'. That the right way? And then he got to know.

Notes

1 *All* is /a/ (e.g. l. 13).
2 Niddrie, Bingham, Magdalene and Northfields are areas of Edinburgh. *Scheme* (l. 13) is a housing estate.
3 (a) *yins* (l. 6) = ones.
  (b) *right strong* (l. 14) = very strong.
  (c) *laddies* (l. 20) = boys.
  (d) *fae* (l. 30) = from.
4 (a) *think on* (l. 31) = think about.
  (b) *yet* (l. 33) = still.
  (c) *wee* (l. 37) = small.
  (d) *keeking* (l. 37) = peering.
5 (a) *we were gone to our bed* (l. 38) = we had gone to bed.
  (b) *done* (l. 39) = did.
  (c) *we'd to* (l. 40) = we had to.
  (d) *feared* (l. 42) = frightened.
  (e) *lassie* (l. 44) = girl.
  (f) *afore, atween* (l. 41 and 47) = before, between.
  (g) *awful old the now* (l. 49) = very old now.

Suggestions for using the book

In what follows we assume that readers have a copy of the cassette which is available with the book. If they have not, we would urge them to obtain one, as its possession will increase significantly the value of the book to them.

The suggestions that we make are addressed primarily to teachers, but individual readers, working through the book on their own, can also benefit from them. If they think of themselves as both teacher and student, they should be able to do most of the things that we suggest, doing the exercises and checking their understanding against our transcripts and analyses.

Just what is done with the book and recordings will depend among other things on whether the readers are British or Irish, whether they are native speakers of English and, if not, what is the standard of their English, the standard of English of the learners and on the use to which they intend to put their new knowledge. For this reason alone it is impossible for us to say what *should* be done. What we can do, however, is to suggest what *might* be done, based on our experience of using these materials with students of various backgrounds. Instructors can then select from our suggested exercises, modify them, and doubtless add to them, in whatever way they feel is appropriate to their particular teaching situation.

We suggest a number of activities: working with the main recordings; completing exercises based on a reading of the book; working with shorter additional recordings.

1. Working with the main recordings

(a) Comprehension

Most students in our experience are attracted by the challenge of trying to understand the tape recordings. But it is important, we think, that the task set them should not be beyond their ability. Instructors will have to decide how much information and other help they need to give to particular groups of students. There is no need to use the recordings in the order in which they appear on the tape. As can be seen, we have made a geographical progression north and then across to Ireland, and in general the accents tend to become increasingly different from RP.

This does not take into account, however, the broadness of accent of our speakers. For example, the Bristol speaker (who has not such a strong accent) may be easier to understand than the speaker from London (whose accent is quite strong), even though, phonologically at least, London speech is closer than Bristol speech to RP. Almost certainly the most difficult recording for everyone will be the one of the Scottish schoolboy. Students can be given a recording, or part of a recording and be required to:

(a) give the general sense of what they hear
(b) answer comprehension questions set by the instructor
(c) transcribe orthographically passages from the recording. This exercise compels students to concentrate hard and makes them recognize just what they understand and what they do not.

(b) Analysis

In trying to understand what is said, presumably the learners must carry out some kind of informal analysis. But as an activity in itself, analysis probably best follows comprehension exercises.

(a) The instructor can ask for general observations on the accent (grammatical and lexical matters are perhaps most usefully treated separately).
(b) A check can be made to discover how general the noticed features are and whether they form part of a pattern.
(c) The analysis arrived at in the class can be compared with ours.

Where there are differences, the recording can be examined for further evidence. The stage at which the word list recordings are introduced into these activities will presumably depend on the nature and level of the students concerned, as well as on the time available. (d) For some students it may be appropriate to attempt phonetic or phonological transcriptions of the tapes.

2. Exercises based on the text

We have set exercises on all of the chapters of the book which are intended to help readers to both check and reinforce their learning. Most of the answers will be found in the text, though we have added notes on one of the exercises.

Chapter 1

1. If English is not your native language, what causes you the greatest difficulty in understanding spoken British English? Try to relate your answer to what you have read in Chapter 1.

If English *is* your native language, are there accents or dialects which you find difficult to understand? If so, can you say why?

2. For another language that you know (possibly your own).

(a) can you give examples of:

   (i)   differences in pronunciation, grammar and vocabulary between people in different regions of a country where the language is spoken?
   (ii) differences in pronunciation and vocabulary between people of different social class?
   (iii) forms of language that are generally thought to be 'incorrect'?

(b) (i)   Is there a region whose accent or dialect is regarded as in some sense inferior?
    (ii) Is there a region whose accent or dialect is regarded as in some sense superior?
    (iii) On what basis are claims made for their inferiority or superiority? Are these claims valid?

3. In the light of your answers to the previous question, compare the language you have taken your examples from with British English.

4. What would your response be to the suggestion that the following are wrong in some way?

> *spud* (for potato)
> *ouse* (for house)
> *im* (for him)
> *I never* (for I didn't)
> *I've seen him only yesterday*
> *There's two of us*
> *happen* (for perhaps)
> *cheers* (for thank you)

(There are notes on this exercise at the end of the section.)

Chapter 2

1. Give an example of each of the following in non-standard English:

(a) multiple negation with two negatives
(b) multiple negation with three negatives
(c) another form of negation found only in non-standard dialects
(d) past tense and past participle with the same form (where this is not the case in Standard English)
(e) present tense, past tense and past participle with the same form.

2. Where are you likely to hear native speakers in Britain saying:

(a) *He smoke a lot*
(b) *I likes it*
(c) *He dos it all the time, do he?*
(d) *I've nae had the chance*
(e) *Where's thine?*
(f) *Give 'n to we*
(g) *Where's that pipe? Ah, there he is.*
(h) *Does he not want to go?*
(i) *He gave it the girl*
(j) *It needs altered.*

3. What non-standard equivalents are there for *who* in the following sentence?

   That's the woman who danced with him.

4. Provide the Standard English equivalents of the following:

(a) *He's the most quickest player we have*
(b) *He does hisself a disservice.*
(c) *He played real good.*

Chapter 3

1. Fill the gaps in the following:

(a)   Clear [l] and dark [ł] are .... of the same phoneme. Some RP speakers use a .... in place of dark [ł] in some environments.

(b)   Some RP speakers make a distinction in pronunciation between *saw* and *sore*. They have one more vowel .... than other RP speakers. This is an example of .... variability.

(c)   When different speakers use a different series of phonemes in pronouncing the same word, we speak of .... variability. An example is the pronunciation of the word *suit*, which may be pronounced with or without /j/.

(d)   When different speakers pronounce the same phoneme in different ways in the same phonological environment, we speak of .... variability.

2. Name as many factors as you can which help to account for variability within RP.

3. What are the voiced equivalents of.

   /p/ /t/ /k/
   /f/ /θ/ /š/ /s/
   /č/

4. How is the glottal stop used in RP?

5. When is /h/ likely to be dropped in RP?

6. Comment on the RP pronunciation of the nasals in the words *cotton* and *symphony*.

7. (e examples of linking /r/ and intrusive /r/.

8. Fill the gaps in the following:

(a) There is an increasing tendency for the final vowel in words like *university* to have a vowel more like / / than the traditional / /.

(b) In some unstressed syllables (such as the first syllable of *believe*), there is a growing tendency for / / to be replaced by / /.

(c) There is variability between /æ/ and /ɑ:/ in such words as .... and ....

(d) Most words that were once pronounced with /uə/ (for example, ... and ....) are now pronounced with / / by most speakers.

(e) There is a growing tendency for the vowel in words like *do* and *you* to become ....

9. Give examples of smoothing and levelling in RP.

Chapter 4

1. Fill the gaps in the following:

(a) Some speakers in the north of England do not distinguish between pairs of words like *look* and *luck,* having the vowel / / in both. However, other (particularly older) northern speakers have / / in *look* but / / in *luck.*

(b) In north of England accents, the words *brass* and *plant* are pronounced with / /.

(c) In most of the north of England, the final vowel of words like *city* is / /. Exceptions to this are L .... , H .... , and T ....

(d) Post-vocalic /r/ survives in the .... of England, central .... , and ....

(e) Scottish speakers make no distinction between *pull* and .... , or between *cot and* ....

(f) While /h/ is variably absent in most regional accents in England and Wales, it is retained in the .... of England, including the city of ....

2. Describe the use of the glottal stop in different parts of the British Isles.

3. In what ways does the pronunciation of *ng* in the words *singer* and *breaking* vary in the British Isles?

4. Where are you likely to hear the word *beautiful* pronounced without /j/?

Chapter 5

Note: Questions relate to the accent and dialect of the city or area referred to in the section title.

I LONDON

1. Fill the gaps in the following:

(a)   The consonant in the middle of the word *water* may be realized as [ ], rather than as [t].

(b)   The initial sound in *thin* and the final sound in *breath* may be / /, rather than / /.

(c)   The second consonant in *bother* and the final consonant in *bathe* may be / /, rather than / /.

(d)   Initial /p, t, k/ are heavily ....

2. Describe the difference between the pronunciation of *paws* and *pause*.

3. In what phonological environments is /l/ realized as a vowel? What effect does this vocalization have on preceding vowels.

II NORWICH

1. What is noteworthy about the pronunciation of the word *few* in Norfolk?

2. Give examples of words which are homonyms in RP but which are quite distinct in Norwich.

3. Give an example of homonyms in Norwich speech which are distinct in RP.

4. How is *-ing* (in, for example, *walking*) pronounced?

III BRISTOL

1. What is the 'Bristol l'?

2. In what obvious way does the Bristol pronunciation of the word *bard* differ from that of RP?

3. Fill the gaps in the following:

(a) There is no / /–/ / contrast in Bristol speech. The pronunciation of *daft* and *hat* illustrates this.

(b) The vowel in the word *cup* is [ ]. In Bristol there seems not to be a / /–/ / contrast.

IV SOUTH WALES

1. In what way does /l/ differ from RP?

2. Fill the gaps in the following:

(a) The vowel in words like *bird* exhibits .... (two words).

(b) Between vowels, when the first vowel is stressed, consonants may be ....

(c) /æ/ and /ɑ/ are distributed largely as in the north of England, but are normally distinguished by ....

3. In what ways is Welsh English influenced by Welsh?

V WEST MIDLANDS

1. In which ways is the accent northern, and in which ways does it resemble a southern accent?

2. What is the vowel in the word *one*?

3. Indicate the following on a vowel chart: /ɪ/ /iː/ /uː/ /ai/ /ei/ /ou/.

VI BRADFORD

1. Fill the gaps in the following:

(a) The words *grass* and *gas* have the same vowel, which is / /.

(b) The words *custard* and *cushion* have the same initial vowel, which is / /.

(c) The final vowel in words like *city* is / /.

2. Describe the realizations of /ei/ and /ou/.

3. In what way can a Yorkshire accent generally be distinguished from a Lancashire accent?

4. Give a phonemic transcription of *Bradford* as pronounced by someone with a West Yorkshire accent.

VII LIVERPOOL

1. In which ways is the Liverpool accent northern? In which way does it resemble southern English accents?

2. In a description of Liverpool speech, what is the significance of pairs of words like *fare* and *fur*?

3. Fill the gaps in the following:

(a) /p, t, k/ are heavily..................... and in final position may even be realized as ....

(b) /r/ is usually a ....

(c) The word *thing* can be transcribed [   ].

(d) .... is present throughout Liverpool speech and gives it a distinctive quality.

VIII EDINBURGH

1. List the vowels of Scottish English as they are described in this book.

2. Assign each of the words in the word list to one of the vowels you have listed.

3. Comment on the following pairs of words: *watt/what*, *pull/pool*, *tide/tied*.

IX BELFAST

1. In which ways is the vowel Belfast system different from that of Edinburgh?

2. What determines the length of vowels?

3. What consonant may be lost between vowels? Give an example of a word in which this may happen.

4. As in Scottish English, which consonant is present (though variably absent in most urban accents of England and Wales)?

X DUBLIN

1. Fill the gaps in the following:

(a) As in Wales and in Belfast, /l/ is always ....

(b) As in Liverpool English, /p, t, k/ tend to be strongly.................... .

(c) The fricatives / / and / / are often pronounced as dental stops.

(d) As in Scotland, Belfast and south-west England, ... (two words) occurs.

(e) In strong accents / / and / / tend not be distinct, and words like *brother* have / /.

2. Comment on /æ/ and /ɑ:/ in Dublin English.

XI DEVON

1. Which voiceless RP consonants may be voiced in Devon speech? In what linguistic environment?

2. In which way do the vowels in *lace* and *soak* differ from their RP equivalents?

3. Fill the gaps in the following:

(a) *Isn't* and *wasn't* are pronounced .... and ....

(b) The present tense of the verb *to be* for all persons is ....

(c) *Tis* is the equivalent of Standard English ....

XII NORTHUMBERLAND

1. Fill the gaps in the following:

The accent is northern in that the vowel [ ] occurs in both *put* and *putt*, and [ ] occurs in both *daft* and *dance*, but resembles southern accents in that ....

2. By comparison with RP, the accent of Tyneside lacks one vowel. What is it?

3. What is significant about the pronunciation of /l/?

XIII LOWLAND SCOTS

1. Transcribe the following words as they would be pronounced in a broad Lowland Scots accent:

round
harm
wrong
land
do
stone

Notes on exercises

Chapter 1, 4

All are perfectly appropriate (and so not 'wrong') in the right circumstances: *spud* is colloquial Standard English; the absence of /h/ is a common feature of regional accents, including cockney (Chapter 5, I); in unstressed syllables /h/ is also frequently absent in RP (Chapter 3); *I never* is a feature of regional dialects (Chapter 2); the co-occurrence of present perfect and definite past time reference seems to be on the increase in Standard English (Chapter 1); *there* plus singular verb with plural complement is quite usual in informal Standard English; *happen* meaning *perhaps* is found in northern dialects (see Chapter 5, VI); *cheers* is increasingly used to mean *thank you* in informal Standard English – young people may be heard saying, for instance, *Cheers for calling* (at the end of a telephone conversation).

3. Using the additional recordings

There are thirteen additional recordings to be found at the end of the tape. These are provided to allow readers to test their ability to recognize and understand regional speech, and should be left until all the transcribed and annotated recordings have been worked through.

The first ten of the additional recordings, which are very brief, exemplify the accents found in some of the main recordings. Students may be asked to identify each accent and to justify their choice. They can also be asked to make transcriptions.

The final three recordings are rather longer. These represent accents which, though they are not treated in Chapter 5, can be identified using the information provided in Chapter 4. It is suggested that the first step should be to listen to a recording once or twice to get the general sense of what is being said. Students can then listen again, checking what they hear against the features found in table 4.2 (it should be noted that individual recordings may not contain examples which permit decisions with respect to all of the features). This should in itself be sufficient to identify the approximate source of each recording, but other features of pronunciation treated in Chapter 4 may be used to confirm the identification. There are a number of dialectal features which are also worth noting. It is a useful exercise to compare each accent with the one or ones treated in Chapter 5 that seem closest to it. As with previous recordings, students can be asked to provide orthographic transcriptions in order that they may discover for themselves precisely how much they do and do not understand.

If you listen to the final section of the tape, you will hear first of all the ten short recordings from the varieties exemplified in Chapter 5. This is then followed by the longer recordings of the three new varieties to be identified. The correct identities of the first ten accents are given below (we have inverted the script so that the reader should not learn the order by accident before attempting to identify the accents), followed by notes on the five new varieties.

The first ten additional recordings are in the order: 1, the north-east;
2, Scotland, 3, London; 4, Belfast; 5, South Wales; 6, Liverpool; 7,

Notes on recordings 11–13

The following brief notes are not exhaustive as we have concentrated
on the main identifying features only, in each case.

11. The first of the three recordings displays the following features:
the vowel in *blood, up*, etc. is /ʊ/ not /ʌ/; the first vowel in *basket* is /æ/
not /ɑː/; the final vowel in words like *journeys* is /ɪ/; /h/ is variably
absent; *bring* is /brɪŋg/; there is no /r/ in words like *poor*; a diphthongal pronunciation of /ei/ is found in *train, table, strange* etc.; *one* is
/wɒn/ (see p. 55). This is sufficient to identify the speaker as being
from the north-west Midlands (in fact she is from Manchester). The
accent in Chapter 5 probably closest to this is that of Bradford; note
in particular that in both cases /r/ is a flap, /t/ is often realized as a
glottal stop, and /ai/ is realized as [ae]. There are also some similarities with Liverpool and West Midlands. Note the use in the north of
Britain of *right* as an intensifier (see p. 119): *right high up = very high
up*.

12. The second recording displays the following features: /ʌ/ (realized as [ə]) is found in words like *bucket*; the vowel in words like
plant is /ɑː/; the final vowel in *plenty, properly* etc. is /iː/; /r/ is not
present in words like *heart*; the vowel in *make* is /eː/, while in *day* it is
/ei/ (see p. 82); /h/ is variably absent. This is sufficient to identify the
accent as Welsh. In fact it is a North Welsh accent, the speaker
having been born in Bangor but now living on the island of Angle-
sey. The accent closest to this in Chapter 5 is, not surprisingly, that of
South Wales. Note the following shared features: doubling of the
consonant in *open, apple, adding*; /r/ as a tap; the vocalic nature of
the sound which comes after /n/ in *manure*. In contrast to South
Wales, however, the North Wales recording does not exhibit lip-
rounding on the vowel in words like *first*; /l/ is not clear in all
environments; and /t/ is strongly aspirated.

13. The third recording displays the following features: the vowel in
words like *son* is /ʊ/; the final vowel in *wealthy, army* is /ɪ/; /h/ is
variably absent e.g. *home, husband*; *anything* and *nothing* end with
/ŋg/; the first vowel in *Daisy* is a diphthongal realization of /ei/. This
is sufficient to identify the speaker as being from the north-west

Midlands, as in the second of these recordings, in this case from Derby. Nevertheless, it is possible to distinguish between the two accents. The diphthongs /ou/ and /ei/ are wider in Derby than in Manchester (see p. 64); /r/ is not a flap in Derby (see p. 61). The intonation is also different; the Manchester intonation is somewhat like that of Merseyside; the Derby intonation is more similar to that of the west Midlands. These two examples will serve to remind the reader that it is possible to make finer and finer distinctions between accents of increasingly restricted areas. Note the non-standard *spotless clean* (see p. 29).

Further reading and references

For a detailed description of RP, the reader is referred to A. C. Gimson *An Introduction to the Pronunciation of English*, 5th edition (Arnold, 1994). For an account of changes in the English language, see C. Barber *The English Language: a Historical Introduction* (Cambridge University Press, 1993). G. Brown *Listening to Spoken English* (Longman, 1977) and D. Crystal & D. Davy *Advanced Conversational English* (Longman, 1975) describe how normal conversational English differs from the careful style of English often most familiar to students. J. C. Wells *Accents of English* (Cambridge University Press, 1982) provides a wealth of detail on British Isles accents; and J. Milroy & L. Milroy (eds) *Real English: the Grammar of English Dialects in the British Isles* (Longman, 1993) does the same for grammar. P. Trudgill *The Dialects of England* (Blackwell, 1990) gives information on both Modern and Traditional dialects and accents.

References

Brown, G. 1977: *Listening to Spoken English*, Longman.
Crystal, D. and Davy, D. 1975: *Advanced Conversational English*, Longman.
Giles, H., Ball, S. and Fielding, G. 1975: 'Communication length as a behavioural index of accent prejudice', *International Journal of the Sociology of Language* 6, 73–81.

Gimson, A. C. 1988: *An Introduction to the Pronunciation of English*, 4th edition, Arnold.

O'Connor, J. D. 1973. *Phonetics*, Penguin.

Palmer, F. R. 1974: *The English Verb*, Longman.

Petyt, K. M. 1977: *'Dialect' and 'Accent' in the Industrial West Riding*, Reading University, unpublished PhD thesis.

Trudgill, P. 1974: *The Social Differentiation of English in Norwich*, Cambridge University Press.

————1979: 'Standard and non-standard dialects of English in the United Kingdom: problems and policies', *International Journal of the Sociology of Language*.

Wakelin, M. F. 1972: *English Dialects: an Introduction*, Athlone Press.

Wells, J. C. 1982: *Accents of English*, Vol. 2. Cambridge University Press.

Wells, J. C. 1984: The Cocknification of RP? In Melchers, G., & Johannesson, N. L. (eds) *Non-Standard Varieties of Language*, Almqvist Wiksell International, 198–205.

Index

Note: Because Scottish and Irish English vowel phonemes cannot be compared directly on a one-to-one basis with English English equivalents, they have not been included in the index. The reader is referred to sections, VIII, IX, X and XIII of Chapter 5.